How To...

HARMONIZE ON THE PIANO

A guide for complementing melodies on the keyboard

BY MARK HARRISON

To access audio visit:
www.halleonard.com/mylibrary

Enter Code
7409-9673-6807-8420

ISBN 978-1-5400-5060-1

HAL•LEONARD®

Visit Hal Leonard Online at
www.halleonard.com

Contact us:
Hal Leonard
7777 West Bluemound Road
Milwaukee, WI 53213
Email: info@halleonard.com

In Europe, contact:
Hal Leonard Europe Limited
42 Wigmore Street
Marylebone, London, W1U 2RN
Email: info@halleonardeurope.com

In Australia, contact:
Hal Leonard Australia Pty. Ltd.
4 Lentara Court
Cheltenham, Victoria, 3192 Australia
Email: info@halleonard.com.au

ABOUT THE AUDIO

On the accompanying audio tracks, you'll find demonstrations of most of the music examples in the book. The solo keyboard tracks feature the left-hand part on the left channel, and the right-hand part on the right channel, for easy "hands separate" practice. The full band tracks feature the rhythm section on the left channel and the keyboard on the right channel, so that you can play along with the band. For examples with only a right-hand or left-hand part, this part is on both channels. This is all designed to give you maximum flexibility when practicing! You can gain full access to the audio by going to *www.halleonard.com/mylibrary* and inputting the unique code printed on the first page of this book.

ABOUT THE AUTHOR

Mark Harrison is a professional keyboardist, composer/arranger, and music educator/author based in Los Angeles. He has recorded three albums as a contemporary jazz bandleader (with the Mark Harrison Quintet), and performs regularly throughout Southern California with the Steely Dan tribute band Doctor Wu. Mark's television music credits include "Saturday Night Live," "American Justice," "Celebrity Profiles," "America's Most Wanted," "True Hollywood Stories," and many others. Mark is an endorsed artist/educator for Dexibell keyboards, and a featured performer for Dexibell at NAMM music industry shows.

Mark has held faculty positions at the Grove School of Music and at the University of Southern California (Thornton School of Music). He currently runs a busy online teaching studio, catering to the needs of professional and aspiring musicians worldwide. Mark's students include Grammy-winners, hit songwriters, members of the Boston Pops and L.A. Philharmonic orchestras, and first-call touring musicians with major acts. He has written over thirty music instruction books, as well as various Master Class articles for *Keyboard* and *How To Jam* magazines.

For further information on Mark's educational products, online lessons, and other news, please visit *www.harrisonmusic.com*.

INTRODUCTION

Welcome to *How to Harmonize on the Piano*. If you're interested in finding and playing the right chords to go with your melodies on the piano but were never quite sure how to do it, then you've come to the right place! Whatever your playing level, this book will enable you to *harmonize* your melodies better, as well as help you understand how chords are used to complement melodies in popular songs.

What is *harmonizing* on the piano? For the purposes of this book, we're using the term *harmonizing* to describe the act of choosing chords to go with a given melody. The melody could be from an original composition you're working on, or it could be a pre-existing tune that you're arranging and/or performing. If you're working on a song from a "fake book," then understanding the principles in this book will also help you improve (and sometimes fix) the chord symbols shown on the chart.

Melody harmonization is a creative process that is ultimately guided by your ear, but there are some rules that can help you along the way. First, we'll look at some simple major scale melodies and see how to harmonize them using triads within a major key. We'll start out by choosing a chord to go with each melody note, which is a good way to learn the basics. Then, the next important step is to accommodate multiple melody notes within the same chord, which requires us to learn the concept of *chord rhythm* (how often the chords will change). This is dependent on various factors including how busy or subdivided the melody is, what the tempo and musical style is, and so on. All the examples in the book (including some well-known melodies) are demonstrated in various contemporary piano styles, so you can apply the concepts right away.

After covering the basics, we'll learn how to harmonize melodies with *rhythmic anticipations*. This occurs when melody notes land "ahead of the beat" instead of "on the beat" (common in most contemporary styles). Then, we'll develop techniques for harmonizing in minor keys and see how to use four-part (or *7th*) chords for a more sophisticated result when required. As a lot of today's pop melodies are based on pentatonic scales, we'll also learn how to harmonize pentatonic melodies in major and minor keys. We'll also explore some *modal* and *mixed major/minor* melodies, which occur more often in contemporary pop styles than you might think!

Later, I'll introduce some more advanced techniques to harmonize chromatic and modal melodies, as well as *bass line* and *parallel motion* harmonization, which can really spice up your piano arrangements! Along the way we'll see harmonization excerpts from famous songs such as "Shenandoah," "Amazing Grace," "House of the Rising Sun," and others.

Five complete melodies are harmonized in various contemporary piano styles in the final chapter of the book. The audio for each of these examples includes a "full band mix" with harmonization (for you to play along) and a "melody and drums only" mix (so you can create and play your own chords along with each melody). This is a great way to develop your harmonization chops within these different contemporary styles. Good luck with your harmonizing on the piano!

– Mark Harrison

CHAPTER 1

ADDING BASIC CHORDS TO MELODIES

MAJOR SCALES, KEYS, AND RESOLUTIONS

First of all, we'll take a look at the major scale, which is the fundamental basis of melody and harmony in most popular styles. I recommend you think of this scale in terms of the intervals it contains, as this most closely parallels how your ear relates to the scale (i.e., whole step, whole step, half step, whole step, whole step, whole step, and half step). Here is the C major scale, showing these intervals:

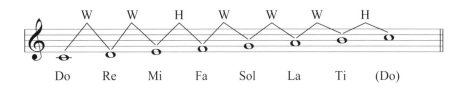

You'll notice that syllables are shown below the C major scale degrees ("Do," "Re," "Mi," etc.). These are known as *solfege* syllables, part of a convenient and recommended labelling system for the notes in any major scale. In other words, we can assign the syllable "Do" to any note, depending on what key we are in. This is referred to as a "moveable Do" application of solfege. This system helps us to understand and vocalize major key melodies, in any key!

Next, we'll look at melodic *resolutions* within the major scale. These are movements between adjacent *active* and *resting* tones and are labelled with the appropriate solfege syllables as follows:

🔊 **Track 1**

On Track 1, you can hear the following resolutions within the C major scale. Do (C) is played as a reference tone before each resolution.

- Re moving to Do (2nd degree moving to 1st degree).

- Fa moving to Mi (4th degree moving to 3rd degree).

- La moving to Sol (6th degree moving to 5th degree).

- Ti moving to Do (7th degree moving to 1st degree).

These resolutions are very natural and predictable sounds, occuring in many famous melodies.

Before we continue, we need to be comfortable with the concept of a *major key*. For example, a song would be in the key of C major if it used a C major scale and if the note C was heard as the *tonic* or home base (i.e., the "Do") of the song. Another quick bit of theory: The *key signature* is a group of sharps or flats at the start of the music, telling us what key we are in. So far, the examples we've seen have no flats and no sharps at the beginning. This means we are in the key of C major. We'll learn more about minor keys later on!

FIRST STEPS: USING MAJOR (PRIMARY) TRIADS

Next, we need to establish some ground rules of harmonization using basic triads (three-part chords) in major keys. Here for your reference are all of the triads available in the key of C major:

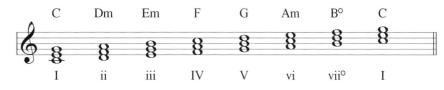

We call these *diatonic* triads in C major, which means they belong to the scale or key. In other words, all of these triads are found within the C major scale and are used within the key of C major. Note the functions (I, ii, iii, etc.) in Roman numerals shown underneath. These refer to the scale degree that each chord is built from, respectively.

Within the above chord options, the I, IV, and V major triads (C, F, and G in this key) are considered *primary triads* as they are the triads most commonly used when harmonizing in simpler styles. They also offer the most basic and definitive ways to harmonize the melodic resolutions seen in Track 1, as we will shortly see. Here's a summary of these primary triads in the key of C major:

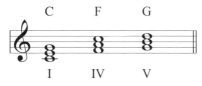

Let's see how to use these three chords to harmonize the notes within a C major scale. To start, we'll pick just one triad for each melody note to keep it simple! The next example shows the suggested primary triad harmonizations for each note within the C major scale.

🔊 **Track 2**

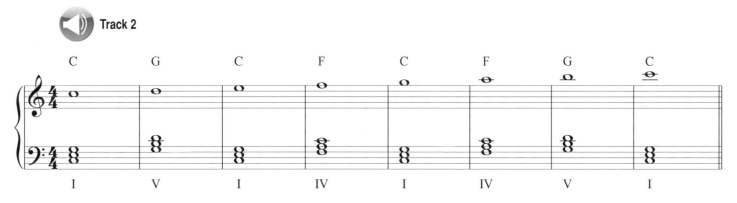

We can analyze each measure of the above example as follows:

- In measure 1, C (Do) is harmonized with the I major triad (C major).

- In measure 2, D (Re) is harmonized with the V major triad (G major).

- In measure 3, E (Mi) is harmonized with the I major triad (C major).

- In measure 4, F (Fa) is harmonized with the IV major triad (F major).

- In measure 5, G (Sol) is harmonized with the I major triad (C major).

- In measure 6, A (La) is harmonized with the IV major triad (F major).

- In measure 7, B (Ti) is harmonized with the V major triad (G major).

- In measure 8, C (Do) is again harmonized with the I major triad (C major).

Again, the solfege syllables help us apply this in every key. For example, in the key of F major, "Do" (which is the note F) would be harmonized with the I major triad (F major), "Re" (which is the note G) would be harmonized with the V major triad (C major), and so on!

Now it's time to look at how to harmonize our first melody with chords. Here's a simple melody in the key of C:

 Track 3

Note that this melody is full of the resolutions within the C major scale that we saw in Track 1:

- From measures 1 to 2, we have A moving to G (this is the 6th scale degree moving to the 5th, or "La to Sol" in this key).

- From measures 2 to 3, we have B moving to C (this is the 7th scale degree moving to the tonic or 1st, or "Ti to Do" in this key).

- From measures 3 to 4, we have F moving to E (this is the 4th scale degree moving to the 3rd, or "Fa to Mi" in this key).

Tip: Many famous traditional and modern songs, as well as national anthems, "Happy Birthday," "Auld Lang Syne," etc. will have these resolutions in their melodies and will use the basic primary major triads in the harmony.

So if we apply the basic "one chord per melody note" harmonization from Track 2 to the melody example in Track 3, we would get the following result.

 Track 4

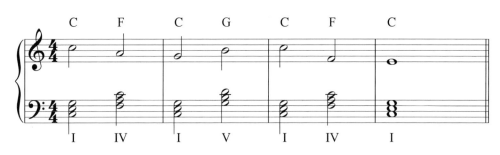

This melody has been harmonized as follows:

- In measure 1 beat 1, C is harmonized with the I major triad (C major).

- In measure 1 beat 3, A is harmonized with the IV major triad (F major).

- In measure 2 beat 1, G is harmonized with the I major triad (C major).

- In measure 2 beat 3, B is harmonized with the V major triad (G major).

- In measure 3 beat 1, C is harmonized with the I major triad (C major).

- In measure 3 beat 3, F is harmonized with the IV major triad (F major).

- In measure 4 beat 1, E is harmonized with the I major triad (C major).

For simplicity, all of the triads in the left-hand part are shown in *root position*, meaning that the root is the lowest note of each chord. For example, in measure 1, the first C major triad has C as its lowest note, then the next F major triad has F as its lowest note. When harmonizing on the piano, this is a good basic approach to begin with!

However, you'll notice that the left-hand part jumps around quite a bit; in other words, we're not moving smoothly from one chord to the next. For a more musical result, the next step would be to use *inversions* of the left-hand triads, to move more smoothly between chords. This is referred to as *voice-leading* and is a staple piano technique in most contemporary styles. First, let's see how the I, IV, and V major triads in the key of C can be inverted as follows:

Track 5

In Track 5, measure 1 begins with the C major triad in root position. Then, the root C is moved up an octave (resulting in E–G–C from bottom to top). This creates a *first inversion* C major triad (meaning the 3rd of the chord is the lowest note). Then, in measure 2, the 3rd of the chord (E) is moved up an octave (resulting in G–C–E from bottom to top). This creates a *second inversion* C major triad (now, the 5th of the chord is the lowest note). Similarly, first and second inversion triads are then shown for the following F and G major triads above.

Next, let's "upgrade" the triad harmonization shown in Track 4, with some of the left-hand triad inversions derived in Track 6, as follows:

Track 6

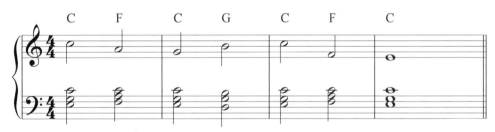

You can hear that the left-hand part now connects more smoothly and "musically" compared to the Track 4 solution we saw earlier.

Next, we'll develop a more contemporary styling for this harmonization. Although it's possible to play these basic chords in the left hand as shown in Tracks 5 and 6, experienced piano players are more likely instead to "voice" the chords below the melody in the right hand. This gives a more modern effect, as follows:

Track 7

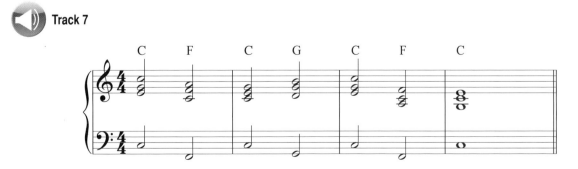

Notice the highest notes in Track 7 are the same as the right-hand melody shown in Tracks 4 and 6, but this time one of the primary triads (C, F or G major) has been inverted below each melody note, per the harmonization first seen in Track 4. The root of each chord is also played by the left hand. This basic setting ("triad-below-melody" in the right hand, with root of each chord in the left hand) is a common foundation in simpler melodic styles. So triad inversions can be used both in the left hand (as in Tracks 5 and 6) and in the right hand (as in Track 7).

Now we'll return to using triads in the left hand below the melody in the right hand, adding some more rhythmic motion and subdivision by using *arpeggios*. An arpeggio occurs when we play the notes of the chord one after another (or *broken chord* style) instead of playing the notes all together. Let's take the basic treatment shown in Track 4 and apply eighth-note arpeggios to this, as follows:

Track 8

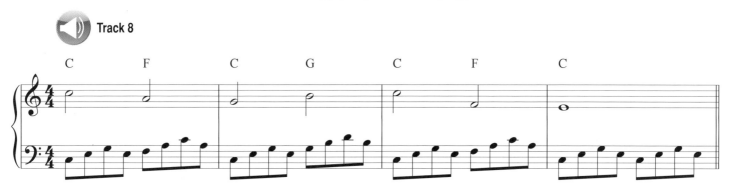

Compared to Track 4, this does add some more motion and interest, however we are still jumping around quite a bit in the left hand as only root position triads are being used. But now we know how to smooth this out, using the inversions from Track 6, as follows:

Track 9

Although still a basic piano setting, this gives a more satisfactory sound compared to Track 8, due to our smoother voice-leading in the left hand.

Before leaving this melody, we'll develop one more left-hand triad arpeggio technique which is commonly used in ballad styles. All of the triads and inversions we have used so far could be described as being *closed*, meaning that their overall span (distance from lowest to highest note) is less than one octave. However, we can transform these into *open triads* by taking the middle note and moving it up by one octave, resulting in an overall span greater than an octave.

Track 10

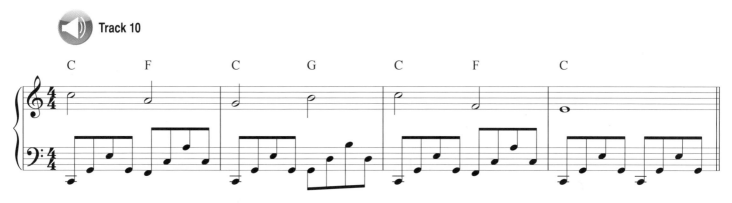

Comparing this example to Track 8, we can see that all of the left-hand triads (still using the basic I, IV, and V chord harmonization) have now been opened, resulting in interval spans greater than an octave for each triad. For example, in measure 1 of Track 10, the left-hand arpeggio C–G–E spells an open C major triad, creating a broader and more professional-sounding result.

A quick tip: As with most piano ballad styles, you will generally depress the sustain pedal for the duration of each chord (and release the pedal at the point of chord change). This also means that you won't need to stretch the left-hand intervals shown in Track 10, as the pedal will take care of the sustain needed within each chord!

ADDING MORE CHOICES: MINOR TRIADS

Now it's time to add some more harmonization choices in major keys (beyond the basic I, IV, and V major primary triads). To do this, we will add the available minor triads. Remember, these are built from the 2nd, 3rd, and 6th scale degrees of the major key. For your reference, here is a summary of all of the major and minor triads in the key of C major:

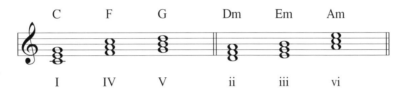

Note that our original I, IV, and V major triad choices are shown in the first measure, and our newly added ii, iii, and vi minor triad choices are shown in the second.

At this stage you may be wondering why we are not including the vii° triad in the choices so far (i.e., B diminished in the key of C major). While this triad is technically available, it has an angular, or *dissonant* sound, and therefore is not commonly used in simpler styles and harmonizations. As a result, for now we'll just stick to the available major and minor triads, which all have a harmonious, or *consonant*, sound quality.

Earlier in Track 2, we established some guidelines for harmonizing the melody notes in the C major scale, with the primary I, IV, and V major triads. Now it's time to expand those harmonization choices by adding in the ii, iii, and vi minor triads, as follows:

Track 11

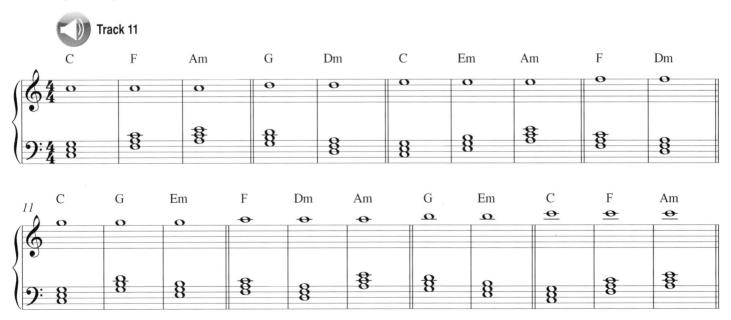

You can see that the harmonization choices have now been expanded for each melody note within the C major scale.

- In measures 1–3, C (Do) can be harmonized with either the I major triad (C major), the IV major triad (F major), or the vi minor triad (A minor).

- In measures 4–5, D (Re) can be harmonized with either the V major triad (G major) or the ii minor triad (D minor).

- In measures 6–8, E (Mi) can be harmonized with either the I major triad (C major), the iii minor triad (E minor), or the vi minor triad (A minor).

- In measures 9–10, F (Fa) can be harmonized with either the IV major triad (F major) or the ii minor triad (D minor).

- In measures 11–13, G (Sol) can be harmonized with either the I major triad (C major), the V major triad (G major), or the iii minor triad (E minor).

- In measures 14–16, A (La) can be harmonized with either the IV major triad (F major), the ii minor triad (D minor), or the vi minor triad (A minor).

- In measures 17–18, B (Ti) can be harmonized with either the V major triad (G major) or the iii minor triad (E minor).

- In measures 19–21, C (Do) can again be harmonized with the options shown for measures 1–3.

With these additional triad options, we'll often have several different ways to harmonize a given melody. Often there may be no single "right" or correct solution. Harmonization choices will ultimately be an "ear decision," but I suggest you factor in the following:

- How the melody is resolving (i.e., the movement between the active and resting tones as discussed earlier) and how that is being supported in the harmony.

- The musical style or level of sophistication required. Simpler styles (i.e., basic pop, rock, and country) will often default to the "I–IV–V" harmonization, whereas adding the minor triads will convey a different quality or mood.

Let's now explore some of these options with another melody example to harmonize.

Track 12

We're still using the "one chord per melody note" harmonization technique seen earlier, but now we can use some of the minor triad options outlined in Track 11, as follows:

Track 13

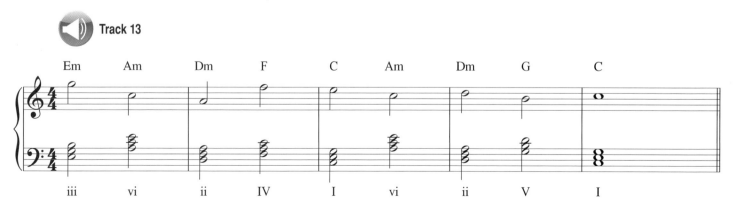

This sounds a little more varied and sophisticated when compared to a basic I–IV–V harmonization (as heard earlier in Track 4). It's important to realize that this is not necessarily better, just different! Of course, you may have a subjective preference for a particular harmonization choice, which is fine. But bear in mind that the harmonies you use will have an important influence on the stylistic perception of your listeners, which may be significant if you are trying to nail a specific musical style or category.

One reason why the previous harmonization works well, is that the movement between some of the chords follows what we call a *circle of 5ths* sequence. In music theory, we define circle of 5ths as a series of "V–I" harmonic relationships. The Em–Am–Dm chord progression is a circle of 5ths sequence. You can test this. Count up five from the last note D (including D) and you reach A. In other words, A is "V of" of D. Count up five from the note A and you reach E, meaning E is "V of" A. The Am–Dm–G–C at the end follows this sequence in a similar way (D is a "V of" G, etc.). These types of chord movements are very common in diatonic triad harmonization.

Next, we'll develop some more piano styles for the harmonization shown in Track 13. As before, a more stylistic result is achieved by inverting the triads below the melody in the right hand (rather than playing them in the left hand), similar to the earlier example shown in Track 7.

Track 14

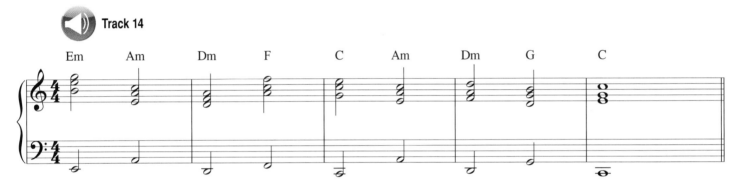

Next, we'll use the left-hand open triad arpeggio technique first seen in Track 10. Each arpeggio consists of the root, 5th, and 3rd of each chord, as follows:

Track 15

Again, in this piano ballad style we're likely to use the sustain pedal for the duration of each chord, to join together and sustain the left-hand arpeggio tones. This will avoid having to stretch out the left-hand intervals, as discussed earlier.

For greater harmonic density and interest, we can combine the left-hand open triad arpeggios from Track 15 with the right-hand, "triad-below-melody" technique from Track 14.

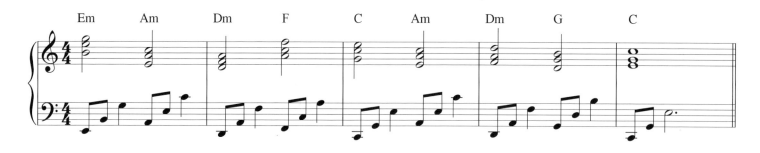

Finally, for this melody example, we can stylize with a more "driving" pop/rock feel with a left-hand, eighth-note root pattern, as follows:

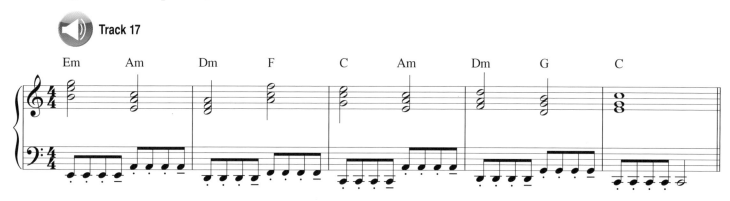 Track 17

Just to recap, all of the melody examples here in Chapter 1 have used a basic "one chord per melody note" harmonization technique, which is a good way for us to get started. However, we'll soon need to accommodate multiple melody notes within each chord, and to develop the important concept of *chord rhythm*, which we're about to do in Chapter 2 next!

For much more information on music theory and harmony basics, please see our *Contemporary Music Theory Level One* and *All About Music Theory* books, both published by Hal Leonard.

CHAPTER 2
USING CHORD RHYTHMS WHEN HARMONIZING

UNDERSTANDING CHORD RHYTHMS

So far when harmonizing melodies, we've been choosing a chord for each melody note, which is a great way to get started! However, unless our melody is very sparse or slow-moving, we'll normally need to accommodate multiple melody notes within each chord.

In this case, the chords will last for a number of beats within each measure. How often the chords change is referred to as the *chord rhythm*, and is an important concept to grasp when harmonizing.

In this section we'll start by harmonizing a basic melody in 4/4 time. This example is still in the key of C major (key signature of no sharps and no flats at the beginning).

🔊 Track 18

Notice the different rhythms used in this melody, including quarter and eighth notes. Most contemporary styles will *subdivide* the beat down to at least the eighth-note level (and many will use 16th-note subdivisions, as we'll look at later on).

Harmonizing by choosing a chord for each melody note (as we did back in Chapter 1) is no longer practical for this busier melody. The chords would change far too often for most stylistic purposes, and the results would be clumsy and distracting. Instead, the chords we choose will have a chord rhythm of their own.

When harmonizing this type of melody in 4/4 time, we should bear in mind the following guidelines:

- Chord changes will normally occur on beat 1 of each measure, or on beats 1 and 3 if there are two chords per measure (beats 1 and 3 are considered the *primary beats*).

- It's less common to need more than two chords per measure, so think carefully before deciding to use more (it may be too busy at faster tempos).

- For melodies in which the eighth note is the smallest subdivision (as in this example) the melody notes landing on beats 1 and 3 are considered more important. They have more harmonic significance than the notes in between, which may be considered as *passing tones*.

- Notes of shorter duration will be less harmonically significant than longer notes or notes which are repeated.

- A busier melody (meaning it has more notes) may need more frequent chord changes than a sparser melody.

- Many melodies in simpler styles will be harmonized with a I chord to begin with, and most melodies will end with this same tonic chord.

USING CHORD RHYTHMS WITH DIATONIC TRIADS

Bearing the above points in mind, and if we were to restrict our harmonization of the above melody to the primary triads (I, IV, and V) in C major, our melody harmonization approach could then be one of the following:

- Look at the melody notes landing on the primary beats in each measure (1 and 3) and see if they are contained within one of the primary triads (i.e., C, F, or G major). If so, we could use this chord for the whole measure.

- If not, look at each melody note landing on the primary beats (1 and 3), and select a primary triad to use for each one (using the earlier harmonization rules from Track 2), resulting in a "two chords per measure" chord rhythm.

Following these guidelines, here's the whole melody with left-hand triad harmonization as follows:

Track 19

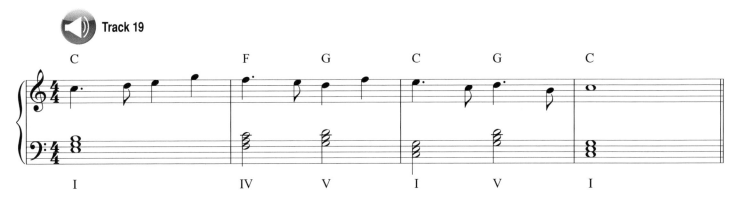

Note that for this first example with multiple melody notes within each chord we have again used simple root position triads in the left hand (as seen earlier in Track 4). The above melody has been harmonized as follows:

- In measure 1, the melody notes on beats 1 and 3 (C and E) are both contained within the I major triad (C major), so this chord can be used for the whole measure.

- In measure 2, the melody notes on beats 1 and 3 (F and D) are not contained within any single primary triad, so we'll need two chords in this measure:

  - The IV major triad on beat 1, to harmonize the note F (see Track 2, measure 4).

  - The V major triad on beat 3, to harmonize the note D (see Track 2, measure 2).

- In measure 3, the melody notes on beats 1 and 3 (E and D) are also not contained in any single primary triad, so we'll again need two chords in this measure:

  - The I major triad on beat 1, to harmonize the note E (see Track 2, measure 3).

  - The V major triad on beat 3, to harmonize the note D (see Track 2, measure 2).

- In measure 4, the melody note on beat 1 (C) is harmonized with the I major triad (C major).

Although the piano treatment of the harmonization in Track 19 is adequate, it sounds a little basic. For a more stylistic result (as seen earlier in Track 7), we could voice the chords below the melody in the right hand, rather than play them in the left hand. This gives a more professional-sounding result, as shown in the example on the next page.

Note that the C major triad in the right hand of measure 1 is used in both first and second inversions, to accommodate the melody notes C and E, on beats 1 and 3, respectively.

Next, we'll develop this piano treatment by adding an open triad arpeggio pattern in the left hand. We first used these left-hand open triad arpeggios back in Track 10, where we derived a "root–5th–3rd" pattern for each chord (C–G–E for the C major chord, F–C–A for the F major chord, etc.). Adding this left-hand treatment to the above triads in the right hand gives us a fuller-sounding piano arrangement.

Again, don't forget to depress the sustain pedal for the duration of each chord. You don't need to stretch the left-hand intervals shown above (the pedal will take care of the sustain needed).

In the harmonization examples shown in Tracks 19–21, we used one chord per measure where possible (i.e., when the melody notes on beats 1 and 3 of the measure, were within the same primary triad), and *only* used two chords per measure when necessary (i.e., when the melody notes on beats 1 and 3 of the measure, were not within the same primary triad). In this case the priority was using the primary triads of the key, and we adjusted the chord rhythm as needed, depending on the melody.

However, we might instead decide to harmonize with two chords per measure throughout, to give greater harmonic movement and interest. In this case, it'll be useful to expand the triad choices beyond the I, IV, and V major triads, by adding the ii, iii, and vi minor triads derived in the last chapter. This will give us harmonic color and variation, while still enabling each melody note landing on a primary beat (beats 1 and 3 in each measure) to be harmonized with a diatonic triad. Here's a quick reminder of all the major and minor triads available, in the key of C major:

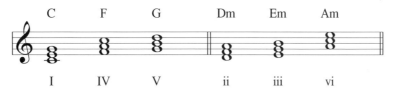

Now that we've added these minor triads into the picture (and assuming a "two chords per measure" chord rhythm throughout), we can harmonize each melody note landing on a primary beat with a diatonic triad, according to the options shown earlier in Track 11.

For example, in measure 1:

- The C on beat 1 could be harmonized with C, F, or Am triads (see Track 11, measures 1–3).

- The E on beat 3 could be harmonized with C, Em, or Am triads (see Track 11, measures 6–8).

Similarly, in measure 2:

- The F on beat 1 could be harmonized with F or Dm triads (see Track 11, measures 9–10).

- The D on beat 3 could be harmonized with G or Dm triads (see Track 11, measures 4–5).

This process would carry on for the remaining bars. A possible harmonization within the above options is shown below (using basic left-hand, root-position triads for now).

Track 22

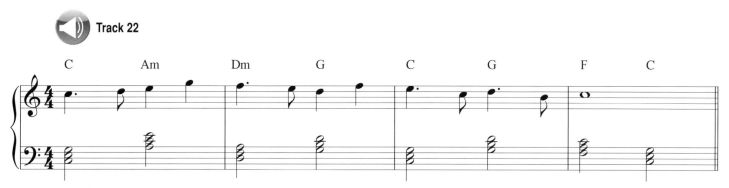

If we compare this to the first primary triad harmonization of this melody in Track 19, there is now more color and movement (with the added minor triads and more consistent chord rhythm). Again, this is not necessarily *better*, rather it sounds *different*. Whether it is more or less appropriate will depend on the style and context you are working in.

Although we have focused up to now on melody notes landing on beats 1 and 3 in each measure, when adding in more triad choices (as in Track 22 above) you'll likely be factoring in how "in-between" melody notes blend with the various chord options. This is largely an "ear decision," but you should bear in mind that there's generally more tolerance for tension between melody notes and chords in more sophisticated styles (such as jazz), and conversely less tolerance in simpler styles, such as pop or traditional music.

Staying with the harmonization used in Track 22, we can again place the same triads below the melody in the right hand for a more polished piano arrangement.

Track 23

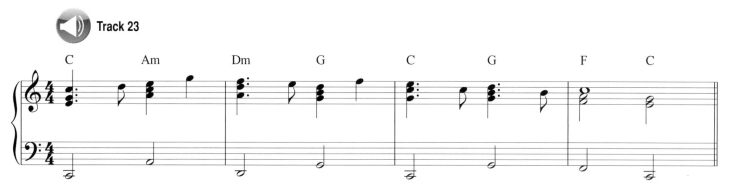

Next, for comparison with the earlier example in Track 21, we can again apply a left-hand open triad arpeggio pattern to the previous harmonization, as shown on the next page.

For much more information on pop ballad piano styles, you should refer to *Pop Piano Book,* published by Hal Leonard.

Melody Harmonization: "Shenandoah"

Next, we'll see how to apply these harmonization techniques to an excerpt from the famous song "Shenandoah," in the key of D major. First, we'll need to be comfortable with the diatonic triads within this key.

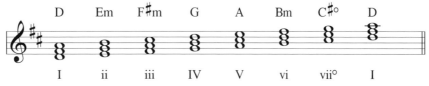

As we saw earlier in the key of C major, although the vii triad (in this case C#° in the key of D) is technically available, in practice it is not commonly used. Again, it's helpful to organize the remaining six diatonic triads into primary (I, IV, and V) and the additional minor triads, which could be termed *secondary* (ii, iii, and vi), as follows:

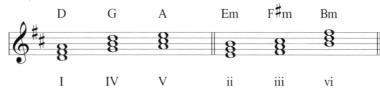

If we limit our harmonization choices to just the primary triads, then some different chord rhythms will be needed to harmonize this melody excerpt (much like we saw earlier in Tracks 19–21).

Track 25

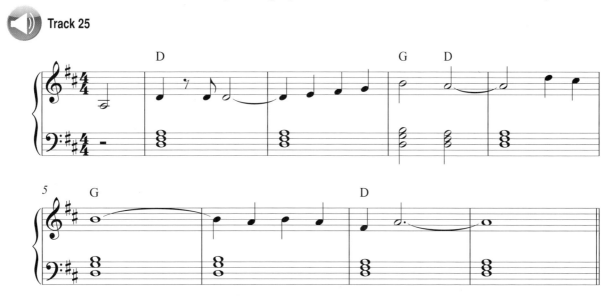

Notice this example has a *pickup* measure. This is the first measure shown, with the melody note of A landing on beat 3. Pickup measures are normally incomplete (i.e., they contain less than four beats, in 4/4 time) and lead into the first complete measure. The pickup measure doesn't normally need to be harmonized, which is why you don't see a chord symbol until the D in the following measure (which is really measure 1 of the musical form).

Let's analyze the melody notes landing on beats 1 and 3 of each measure (following the pickup measure), so we can understand the primary triad choices used for this harmonization.

- In measure 1, the note D lands on beats 1 and 3. So the I major triad (D) is the obvious choice, particularly at the start of the song.

- In measure 2, the note D lands on beat 1 and the note F♯ lands on beat 3. As these are both within the I major triad (D), we'll continue with this chord.

- In measure 3, the note B lands on beat 1 and the note A lands on beat 3. These are not contained within the same primary triad, so we'll use a IV major (G) on beat 1, changing to a I major (D) on beat 3. The melody here (together with the primary triad restriction) has prompted us to use two chords in this measure.

- In measure 4, the note A continues on beat 1 (tied from the previous measure) and the note D lands on beat 3. Again, these are both within the I major triad (D), so we can continue with this chord, restating it in the left hand.

- In measure 5, the note B lands on beat 1 and lasts for the whole measure. The only primary triad containing B is the IV major triad (G).

- In measure 6, the note B continues on beat 1 (tied from the previous measure) and also lands on beat 3. Again, this note is within the IV major triad (G), so we can continue with this chord.

- In measure 7, the note F♯ lands on beat 1 and the note A lands on beat 2 (and continues through beat 3). These are both within the I major triad (D). Also, this measure is the seventh measure of an eight-measure melodic phrase, which is a very common place to *cadence*, or lead back, to chord I (the tonic) in simpler melodies and styles.

- In measure 8, the note A (tied from the previous measure) lasts for the whole measure, so we can stay on the I major chord (a good option in simpler styles).

If we expand the harmonization choices to include the diatonic minor (or secondary) triads, then a more consistent chord rhythm would be possible for this melody excerpt. Also, we'll see that when using minor chord harmonization, it's normally acceptable for the melody note on the primary beat to be the *7th* of the chord (i.e., not just a basic root, 3rd, or 5th), even in simpler styles. With this in mind, here's the next harmonization for the same "Shenandoah" melody:

Track 26
Backing Track Style: Pop Ballad

Here we see that the harmonization is the same as Track 25, except for measures 3–4, which are harmonized with the vi minor triad (i.e., Bm in this key). Let's look at the melody notes in these two measures in more detail.

- In measure 3, the note B lands on beat 1 and the note A lands on beat 3. Adding in the possibility of the vi minor triad, we see that B is the root and A is the 7th of this chord (implying a Bm7 chord in total). So, we can now use the same chord for the whole measure (rather than change chords on beat 3, as in Track 25).

- In measure 4, the note A continues on beat 1 (tied from the previous measure) and the note D lands on beat 3. These are the 7th and 3rd, respectively, of the vi minor chord (again, implying a Bm7 overall), so we can continue with this chord.

In Track 26, we've also used a sparser, left-hand open triad arpeggio pattern (for example, compared to Track 21 earlier). This leaves more space for the melody to project over the accompaniment.

Melody Harmonization: "Amazing Grace"

Next, we'll harmonize an excerpt from another famous song, "Amazing Grace," in 3/4 time. This in the key of G major, and as before we'll start with primary triad harmonization. Again, we'll need to be comfortable with the diatonic triads in this key.

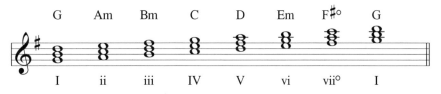

We can identify the primary major triads (I, IV, and V) and the secondary minor triads (ii, iii, and vi) in this key, as follows:

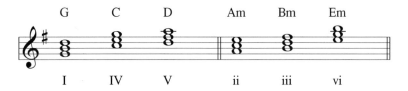

Here's our first harmonization of the "Amazing Grace" melody excerpt, limited to primary triads:

Track 27

We see this example also has a pickup measure, containing the melody note D, which leads into the first measure of the form. The measure numbers referenced in the bullet points on the next page, again exclude this pickup measure. The left-hand part consists of the triads I, IV, and V, this time using inversions for a smooth chord progression.

In previous examples in 4/4 time, we've focused on the melody notes landing on the primary beats (beats 1 and 3 in 4/4 time). However, in 3/4 time (unless the tempo is very slow), beat 1 is the *only* primary beat. In other words, the melody note landing on beat 1 is of the most significance when harmonizing. We'll also keep an eye on melody notes landing on beat 3, as this may help with harmonization choices. With this in mind, we can analyze the chords used in Track 27 as follows:

- In measure 1, the note G lands on beat 1. The I major triad (G) is the obvious choice, particularly at the start of the song.

- In measure 2, the note B lands on beat 1. This is still within the I major triad (G), so we can continue with this chord.

- In measure 3, the note G again lands on beat 1. Technically we could still stay on the I major triad (G), although by the third measure we would normally want to change to a different chord. We notice that the note E is on beat 3 of this measure, and the notes E and G are within the IV major triad (C). C major chord works well here.

- In measure 4, the note D lands on beat 1. This is within the I major triad (G), as well as the V major triad (D). So it's a subjective preference whether we resolve back to the tonic chord (G) as we did here, or instead move to the V chord. Either could work!

- In measure 5, the note G lands on beat 1 (the same as in measure 1). Regardless of our decision in measure 4 above, we're likely to resolve back to (or stay on) the tonic chord of G major at this point, as this measure is the start of a four-measure phrase (i.e., measures 5–8). For simpler melodies, there will be a tendency to use the tonic chord of the key (i.e., G major) at this strong point in the melodic form. This is not a hard and fast rule of course, just a guide!

- For measure 6, see measure 2 comments above.

- In measure 7, the note D lands on beat 1 (and is tied over to measure 8). We could of course still stay on the I major triad (G). Our other choice with D in the melody is the V major triad (D). This leads well back to the tonic chord (G) and, given that the melody continues beyond the excerpt shown here, is our best choice.

You can see that some creative decisions and subjective preferences are on display in this example. I hope these examples will give you a frame of reference within which you can begin making these harmonization choices!

Next, we'll expand the harmonization to consistently use one chord per measure (for greater chord movement), and to include some diatonic minor triads in the key of G. We'll also use right-hand triads below the melody in a 3/4 gospel style. One of various harmonization choices within this expanded palette is shown below.

Track 28
Backing Track Style: 3/4 Gospel

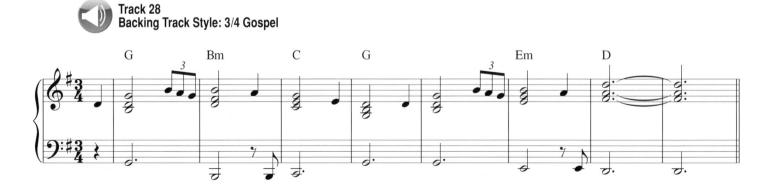

As we saw earlier when harmonizing the melody in C major (Tracks 22–24) the harmonization choices are multiplied when we add in the diatonic minor triad options. Feel free to experiment with the choices available!

RHYTHMIC ANTICIPATIONS: EIGHTH NOTES

Now let's work with a new melody, this time in the key of F major. This melody will feature *rhythmic anticipations,* which are common in many contemporary melodies and styles. We'll need to know how to handle these melodic anticipations when harmonizing.

A simple and very common anticipation occurs when a melody note is half a beat ahead, instead of on the beat. This is known as an *eighth-note anticipation.*

To help understand this concept, I recommend that you become familiar with how eighth-note rhythms are counted, as shown below.

In contemporary music, it's common to refer to beats 1, 2, 3, and 4 as the *downbeats,* while the eighth notes in between (the "&s" shown above) are known as *upbeats.* An *anticipation* occurs when a melody note lands on an upbeat and is tied over to (or followed by a rest on) the following downbeat.

The most common eighth-note anticipations in contemporary styles occur ahead of primary beats (i.e., beats 1 and/or 3 in a 4/4 measure). Here's an excerpt from the upcoming melody in the key of F, demonstrating this principle:

Track 29

On the left in measures 1–2, we're using simple half-note and whole-note rhythms, with everything landing on the beat. However, in measures 3–4, the melodic motif from measures 1–2 has been re-phrased as follows:

- In measure 3, the note E lands on the "&" of beat 2, halfway through beat 2, *anticipating* (landing ahead of) beat 3 of this measure.

- In measure 3, the note C lands on the "&" of beat 4, halfway through beat 4, anticipating beat 1 of measure 4. If you listen to Track 29, you'll hear that the first half sounds quite static and ordinary, whereas the second half sounds more rhythmically lively and interesting. This is due to the rhythmic anticipations used in the melody.

So why is this concept important when harmonizing melodies? Well, melody notes that anticipate primary beats can be considered as "belonging to" those primary beats for harmonization purposes. This is best demonstrated by looking at the next melody example, in the key of F major.

As you can see, the beginning of this melody is similar to measures 3–4 of Track 29. This melody contains anticipations of beat 3 in every measure, and anticipations of beat 1 in bars 2 and 4.

When harmonizing this melody, we'll apply the following rules:

- A melody note landing on the "&" of beat 2 (and anticipating beat 3) will be treated as if it were landing on beat 3 for harmonization purposes.

- A melody note landing on the "&" of beat 4 (and anticipating beat 1 of the next measure) will be treated as if it were landing on beat 1 of the next measure, for harmonization purposes.

Once we interpret the melody in this way, we can apply similar harmonization techniques as developed earlier. Just before we do that, let's familiarize ourselves with the diatonic triads in the key of F.

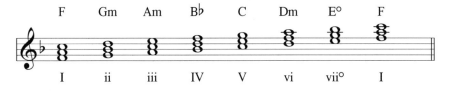

Let's also identify the primary major triads (I, IV, and V) and the secondary minor triads (ii, iii, and vi) in this key.

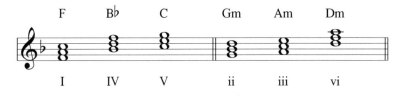

Now it's time to harmonize this melody in F major. Looking at the first three measures, the melody notes landing on the primary beats 1 and 3 (or their anticipations) don't belong to the same primary triad (i.e., F, B♭ or C major). So, if the priority was to use primary triad harmonization, we would need the following "two chords per measure" approach (except in measure 4):

Track 31

Here, the left hand is playing triad inversions to voice lead between chords (similar to previous examples in Tracks 25 and 27). Notice that the left-hand triads are still landing on beats 1 and 3, even though the right-hand melody is often anticipating these beats. In real-world contemporary styles, melodic anticipations frequently don't impact upon chord rhythms.

We could again create a more stylistic piano arrangement by voicing the chords below the melody in the right hand, instead of playing them in the left hand. When applying this treatment to a melody with anticipations, the right-hand triads can anticipate along with the melody, while the left hand can still play the chord root on beats 1 and 3 of each measure.

Track 32

In this piano style, the right hand is essentially anticipating the left hand for most of the chords. This often occurs in contemporary pop and ballad styles.

Next, we'll stylize this harmonization in a pop/rock piano setting, by adding some eighth-note pickups in the left-hand part, as follows:

Track 33
Backing Track Style: Pop/Rock

This piano part is the same as in Track 32, except that we have rearticulated some chord roots on the "&" of beat 2 of each measure, leading into beat 3. This is a very common rock piano technique.

For much more on pop/rock piano styles, please see our *Pop Piano Book* and *Beginning Rock Keyboard* books, both published by Hal Leonard.

Next, we'll harmonize the melody from Track 30 with a mix of primary major triads (I, IV, and V) and secondary minor triads (ii, iii, and vi). Here's a quick reminder of these diatonic triads, in the key of F major:

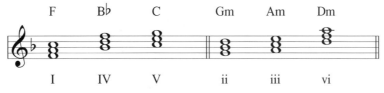

In the following treatment, we'll again use two chords per measure in measures 1–3, and (as before) the anticipated melody notes will be treated as if they were landing on the primary beats for harmonization purposes. Adding these minor triads into the mix, we now have various diatonic triad options for our harmonization of each melody note from Track 30.

In measure 1:

- The F on beat 1 could be harmonized with F, B♭, or Dm triads.

- The E anticipating beat 3 could be harmonized with C or Am triads.

Similarly, in measure 2:

- The D anticipating beat 1 could be harmonized with B♭ or Gm triads.

- The A anticipating beat 3 could be harmonized with F, Dm, or Am triads.

This process can now continue for the rest of the melody, using similar principles as shown in Track 11, but transposed to the key of F. One of various choices within these options is shown below (with left-hand triad inversions for voice leading).

Track 34

Again, notice that the right-hand melody is anticipating the left-hand chords. You are encouraged to experiment with the various diatonic triad choices available for this melody!

Now we'll voice these chords below the melody in the right hand, with the left hand playing the chord roots on beats 1 and 3 of each measure (similar style to Track 32).

Track 35

Next, we'll play this harmonization in a pop/rock piano style, this time with the left hand playing a consistent quarter-note pulse below the right-hand anticipations.

Track 36
Backing Track Style: Pop/Rock

DIATONIC FOUR-PART (7TH) CHORDS

Now it's time to move beyond triads, by introducing *four-part chord* harmonization for this melody in the key of F. (Four-part chords are also sometimes referred to as *7th chords* because they include the 7th above the root in addition to the 3rd and the 5th). Four-part chords sound denser and more sophisticated compared to the triads (or three-part chords) we've used so far. Let's start out by reviewing the diatonic four-part chords in the key of F major.

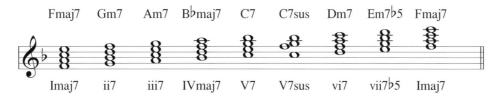

You'll see that two alternate versions are shown for the V chord here. The C7 (*dominant 7th*) chord has a more traditional sound and leads back strongly to the tonic or I chord of the key. The C7sus (suspended dominant 7th) is a smoother, pop-friendly sound which has a less leading quality. Both are commonly used, depending on the musical style and context.

As for diatonic triads, the vii chord here (in this case Em7♭5) is not often used in the contemporary styles, leaving the remaining (i.e., I through VI) diatonic four-part chords as the commonly used options.

For more information on four-part chord spelling and diatonic four-part chords, please see *Contemporary Music Theory Level One* published by Hal Leonard. For more information on dominant and suspended chords and dominant-to-tonic relationships, please read *Contemporary Music Theory Level Two*, also published by Hal Leonard.

A simple way to introduce four-part chord harmonization would be to expand *all* of the diatonic triad choices used in Track 34–36 to their corresponding four-part chords. In other words, we could use Dm7 instead of the Dm triad, Am7 instead of the Am triad, and so on. To begin with, we'll play basic, root-position four-part chords in the left hand to accompany the melody in the right hand.

Track 37

Moving four-part chords around in root position in this way is rather basic of course. We're just illustrating the harmonization to begin with. A somewhat smoother result is obtained by using four-part chord inversions and voice leading in the left hand, as follows:

Track 38

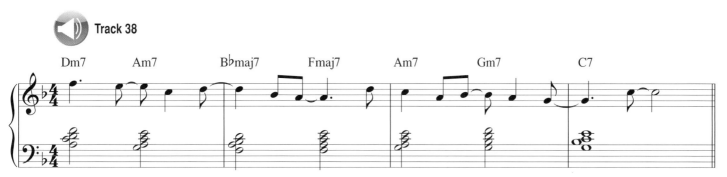

Earlier we saw in various harmonizations using triads (Tracks 20, 24, 28, etc.) that a more professional-sounding result was obtained by inverting the triads below the melody in the right hand. Although this is also possible with four-part chords, in practice a better result is often achieved by "splitting off" the upper part of the chord (i.e., the 3rd, 5th, and 7th, which together form a triad) and then inverting these *upper triads* below the melody, while still playing the root of the overall chord in the left hand. Take a look at how these upper triads would be created for the commonly used diatonic four-part chords in F major.

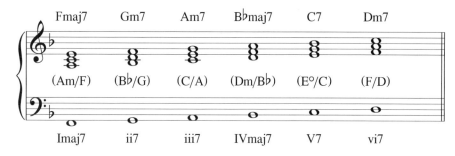

Comparing this panel to the previously shown diatonic four-part chords in F, we see that the commonly used chords (I through VI) are now split so that the root is in the bass clef and the upper tones (3rd, 5th, and 7th) are in the treble clef. These upper tones by themselves form a triad in each case. Note the *composite* chord symbols (root note followed by a suffix) are shown above the treble staff, and the corresponding *slash* chord symbols (showing a triad placed over a bass note) are below the treble staff.

You're much more likely to see the composite chord symbols (rather than the corresponding slash chord symbols) in a chart or fake book. However, being able to "voice" four-part chords on the piano in this way, will make your playing sound more professional! Next, we'll take the four-part chord harmonization used in Tracks 37–38, derive the upper triads as shown above, and then invert these triads below the melody (while keeping the original chord roots in the bass register), as follows:

 Track 39

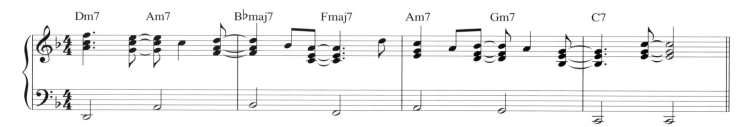

This upper triad technique will work when the 3rd, 5th, or 7th of the four-part chord is the melody note being harmonized (which will very often be the case). When the root is in the melody (as seen in the second half of measure 4 above), we can simply use the basic triad form of the chord (i.e., the C major triad).

Let's look at these voicing choices in more detail.

In measure 1:

- The melody note F on beat 1 was harmonized with a Dm7 chord in Tracks 37–38. The "upper triad" of the Dm7 chord is F major, which is inverted below the F in the melody and placed over the chord root of D in the bass clef.

- The melody note E anticipating beat 3, was harmonized with an Am7 chord in Tracks 37–38. The "upper triad" of the Am7 chord is C major, which is inverted below the E in the melody and then placed over the chord root of A in the bass clef.

In measure 2:

- The melody note D anticipating beat 1, was harmonized with a B♭maj7 chord in Tracks 37–38. The "upper triad" of the B♭maj7 chord is D minor, which is inverted below the D in the melody and placed over the chord root of B♭ in the bass clef.

- The melody note A anticipating beat 3, was harmonized with a Fmaj7 chord in Tracks 37–38. The "upper triad" of the Fmaj7 chord is A minor, which is inverted below the A in the melody and then placed over the chord root of F in the bass clef.

In measure 3:

- The melody note C on beat 1 was harmonized with an Am7 chord in Tracks 37–38. The upper triad of the Am7 chord is C major, which is inverted below the C in the melody and placed over the chord root of A in the bass clef.

- The melody note B♭ anticipating beat 3, was harmonized with a Gm7 chord in Tracks 37–38. The upper triad of the Gm7 chord is B♭ major, which is inverted below the B♭ in the melody and then placed over the chord root of G in the bass clef.

In measure 4:

- The melody note G anticipating beat 1, was harmonized with a C7 chord in Tracks 37–38. The "upper triad" of the C7 chord is E diminished, which is inverted below the G in the melody, and then placed over the chord root of C in the bass clef (this upper diminished triad sounds weak in root position, but is acceptable when inverted).

- As mentioned earlier, the melody note C anticipating beat 3, is harmonized with a C major triad.

This example introduced us to the important concept of upper triad voicings. Much more about this important technique in Chapter 3!

Next, we'll take this melody and harmonization, and stylize it in a Hall & Oates pop/rock piano style, as follows:

Track 40
Backing Track Style: Pop/Rock

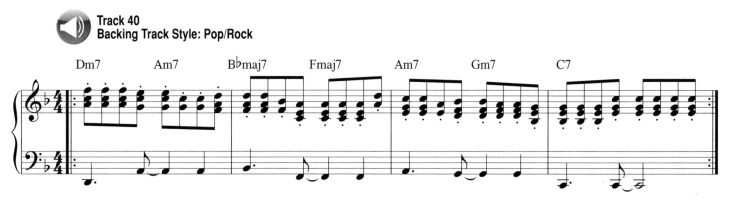

In comparison to Track 39, this piano treatment has the following characteristics:

- The melody notes (with the supporting upper triads) are repeated on every eighth note instead of the durations originally shown in Track 30.

- The left-hand bass notes are anticipating beat 3 instead of landing on beat 3. This means that the *whole chord change* is now anticipated (instead of the more typical right hand anticipating the left-hand part).

When first looking at the diatonic four-part chords in the key of F, we saw there were two alternate forms of the V (five) chord which were available: the dominant 7th (C7) and the suspended dominant 7th (C7sus). So next, we'll vary the upper triad treatment from Track 39, by suspending the dominant chord harmonization as follows:

Track 41

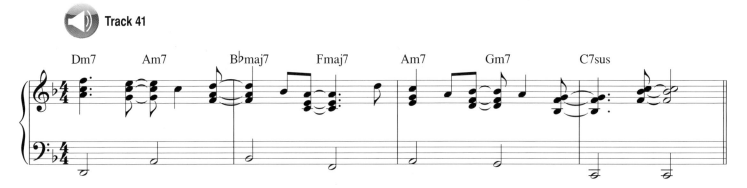

Note that on the C7sus chord, instead of using an upper triad in the right-hand part, we're adding the suspended 4th (F) as well as the 7th (B♭) below the melody notes of G and C. These are the critical chord tones which help define the suspended dominant to our ear. This suspended dominant is a smoother and more pop-friendly sound compared to the more traditional C7 chord voicing used in Track 39. More to come about suspended dominant voicings in Chapter 3!

For much more information on dominant and suspended dominant chords, please see our *Contemporary Music Theory Levels One and Two* books, published by Hal Leonard.

Finally, for the above melody and harmonization in the key of F, we'll create a pop/rock piano part with a more active left-hand pattern in *swing eighths*. This rhythmic style divides pairs of eighth notes in a "two-thirds to one-third" ratio, rather than exactly "half and half" as with regular (*straight*) eighths.

Track 42
Backing Track Style: Pop/Rock Shuffle

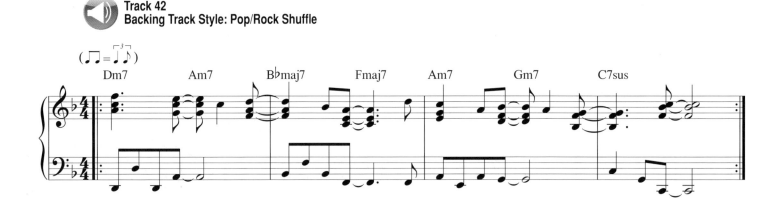

In comparison to Track 41, this piano treatment has a busier left-hand pattern, playing roots and 5ths of chords leading into the anticipation of beat 3 in each measure.

MINOR SCALES AND KEYS

Now we'll look at how to harmonize a melody in the key of A minor. This key is *relative* to the key of C major (it shares the same key signature; no sharps and no flats). Theory note: The relative minor key is "built from" the 6th degree of the corresponding major key. In Chapter 1, we saw that the 6th degree of the C major scale is the note A, so the keys of C major and A minor are relative to one another and share the same key signature.

OK, so here's where it can get a little tricky! We just had one major scale to deal with in a major key (for example, in Chapter 1, our melodies were within the C major scale, in the key of C major). But, in a minor key, the melodies we're harmonizing could use up to *three* different minor scales! In the key of A minor, we could encounter the following scales in the melody:

A Natural Minor

A Harmonic Minor

A Melodic Minor

As you can see, these three scales are similar, except for the different *6th* and *7th* degrees.

The bottom line is this: If we are in a minor key, then the minor key signature will give us a *natural minor* scale (which is commonly used for contemporary melodies in minor keys). If our melody makes use of the other minor scales (i.e., the different 6th and 7th scale degrees shown above), then we need to "top up" the key signature with *accidentals* (either sharps or naturals to cancel out flats in the key signature). We'll see this in some of the upcoming melody examples in minor keys.

For much more information on minor scales, keys and key signatures, please see our *Contemporary Music Theory Level One* book, published by Hal Leonard.

When harmonizing simple melodies in minor keys, we can start out with diatonic triads, much like we did for major keys. The various triad options from the previously shown A minor scales can, in practice, most often be simplified as follows:

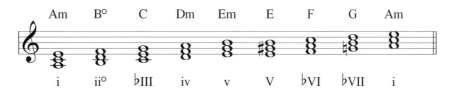

Note that all of these triads are contained within (diatonic to) the A natural minor scale, except for the E major triad which is within the A harmonic and melodic minor scales. The E major triad is included so we can harmonize the melody note of G♯ (which can occur in this key), and to lead back more strongly to the i minor chord as needed.

We saw previously in major keys that the vii° triad (i.e., B° in the key of C major) was not commonly used, due to its dissonant sound. Similarly, the diminished triad shown above (again B°, this time the ii chord in the key of A minor) is not widely used.

Melody Harmonization: "Greensleeves"
With all the above in mind, let's harmonize an excerpt from the famous minor-key melody "Greensleeves," using a chord rhythm of "one chord every two measures," and the diatonic triads from the key of A minor derived earlier.

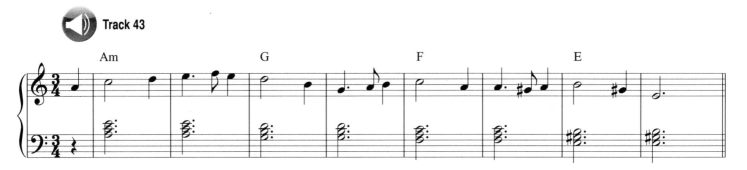

Note that even though we are in the key of A minor, this melody excerpt contains the note G♯. This is evidence that the melody uses the A harmonic and/or A melodic minor scales (rather than being limited to the A natural minor scale, which is what the key signature of no sharps and no flats gives us). We will need to take this into account when harmonizing the melody.

As discussed earlier, in 3/4 time there is normally only one primary beat per measure, on beat 1. So here we look at beat 1 of each measure to see which diatonic triads (in the key of A minor) the melody notes belong to. If the melody notes landing on beat 1 of consecutive measures (for example, on beat 1 of both measures 1 and 2) are within the same diatonic triad, we might then use that triad to harmonize those two measures, therefore enabling the "one chord every two measures" chord rhythm as used here. We can further analyze the relationship of the melody to the diatonic triad harmonization used shown below (measure numbers exclude the pickup measure).

In measures 1 and 2:

- The melody notes landing on beat 1 of these measures are C and E respectively. These are both within the A minor triad, which is a good starting choice (the tonic, or i, minor chord of the key).

In measures 3 and 4:

- The melody notes landing on beat 1 of these measures are D and G respectively. These are both within the G major triad (♭VII).

In measures 5 and 6:

- The melody notes landing on beat 1 of these measures are C and A respectively. These are both within the F major triad (and A minor triad). F major is a good choice here as we've already recently used the tonic A minor chord, and it continues the "descending" direction of the harmony so far.

In measures 7 and 8:

- The melody notes landing on beat 1 of these measures are B and E respectively. These are both within the E major triad and E minor triads. However, the E major triad (V) is preferred here, due to the G♯ in the melody in measure 7 as mentioned above.

Next, we'll change things up by increasing the chord rhythm to "one chord per measure" and use left-hand open triad arpeggios for a 3/4 piano ballad style, as follows:

Track 44
Backing Track Style: 3/4 Ballad

For this busier harmonization, we have various diatonic triad choices (again looking at the melody notes on beat 1 of each measure). Let's look at the first three measures:

- In measure 1, the melody note C is within the A minor, C major, and F major triads.

- In measure 2, the melody note E is within the C major, E minor, and E major triads.

- In measure 3, the melody note D is within the G major and D minor triads.

We can see that multiple choices are available when applying a "one chord per measure" harmonization to this melody (while still ensuring that the melody note on the primary beat is within a diatonic triad). With a traditional melody and eight-measure form such as this though, we're likely to bear the following points in mind:

- As seen earlier in Track 43 when using the "one chord every two measures" harmonization, we'll often start with the tonic, or i, minor chord (A minor), and end the eight-measure phrase with the V chord (E major), which could then lead back to the tonic chord to continue the harmonization.

- The fifth measure of this eight-measure phrase is considered a *strong measure* (particularly as we're now changing chords in every measure). In other words, the chord used here will often refer back to the key in more traditional styles. So the choice of A minor anchors the key here in the middle of this melodic phrase.

Feel free to experiment with the diatonic triad options available for this classic melody!

RHYTHMIC ANTICIPATIONS: SIXTEENTH NOTES

Next, we'll work on another melody in the key of A minor, this time featuring *16th-note* rhythmic anticipations, which are central to many of today's pop and R&B styles. As for the eighth-note anticipations previously discussed, we'll need to know how to handle these 16th-note anticipations when harmonizing melodies.

To help understand this concept, I recommend that you become familiar with how 16th-note rhythms are counted, as follows:

As seen earlier, in 4/4 time, it's typical to refer to beats 1, 2, 3, and 4 as the downbeats.

A 16th-note anticipation occurs when a melody note lands a 16th note ahead of a downbeat and is tied over to (or followed by a rest on) that downbeat.

So for example:

- If a melody note lands on the last 16th note of beat 1 (referred to as the "a of 1") and is tied over to (or followed by a rest on) beat 2, this is a 16th-note anticipation of beat 2.

- If a melody note lands on the last 16th note of beat 2 (referred to as the "a of 2") and is tied over to (or followed by a rest on) beat 3, this is a 16th-note anticipation of beat 3.

Here's an excerpt from the upcoming melody in the key of A minor, demonstrating this principle:

Track 45

Notice this melody excerpt is rhythmically busier than earlier examples, with the use of 16th-note rhythmic subdivisions.

In measures 1–2, we see that the melody is landing on downbeats (i.e., on beats 1, 2, 3, and 4 of the first measure and beat 1 of the second measure). However, in measure 3, the same melodic motif has been rephrased as follows:

- The note E lands on the "a" of beat 1 (the last 16th note of beat 1), and is tied over to beat 2, therefore anticipating beat 2 of this measure.

- The note B lands on the "a" of beat 3 (the last 16th note of beat 3), and is tied over to beat 4, therefore anticipating beat 4 of this measure.

- The note A lands on the "a" of beat 4 (the last 16th note of beat 4), and is tied over to beat 1 of the next measure, therefore anticipating beat 1 of this measure.

If you listen to Track 45, you'll hear that the first half sounds rather "straight-laced" and traditional, whereas the second half sounds more rhythmically interesting. This is due to the 16th-note rhythmic anticipations used in the melody.

When harmonizing melodies with eighth-note anticipations, we were mostly concerned with melody notes which anticipated beats 1 and 3 (in 4/4 time). Now when harmonizing 16th-note melodies, we need to ensure that our chords work with the melody notes landing on all of the downbeats or their anticipations. This is because all beats are essentially primary beats in 16th-note styles.

So for melodies using 16th-note anticipations, melody notes which anticipate downbeats (i.e., beats 1, 2, 3, or 4, in 4/4 time) can be considered as "belonging to" those downbeats for harmonization purposes. Let's demonstrate this by looking at the next melody example, in the key of A minor.

Track 46

As you can see, the beginning of this melody is the same as measures 3–4 of Track 45. This melody anticipates (by a 16th note) beats 2 and 4 in measures 1 and 3, beat 1 in measure 2, and beats 1, 2, and 3 in measure 4.

When harmonizing this melody, we'll treat all 16th-note anticipations of downbeats as if they were landing on the following downbeat for harmonization purposes. Once we interpret the melody in this way, we can apply similar diatonic triad harmonization techniques (within the key of A minor) as developed earlier.

Bearing all the previous points in mind, our 16th-note melody harmonization approach could then be:

- Look at the melody notes landing on the downbeats (or their anticipations) in each measure and see if they are all contained within an available triad in the key of A minor. If so, we could use this chord for the whole measure.

- If not, look at each melody note landing on the downbeats (or their anticipations) in each half of the measure (i.e., look at beats 1 and 2 separately, then beats 3 and 4 separately), and see if each pair of melody notes is contained within an available triad. If so, we can use these chords on beats 1 and 3, respectively (resulting in a "two chords per measure" chord rhythm).

- If the above techniques don't work, we may need to choose chords on a beat-by-beat basis. This is sometimes needed in the 16th-note styles (particularly slower-tempo ballads).

Using these guidelines, let's now harmonize the melody in Track 46 with diatonic triads in the key of A minor, as follows:

Track 47

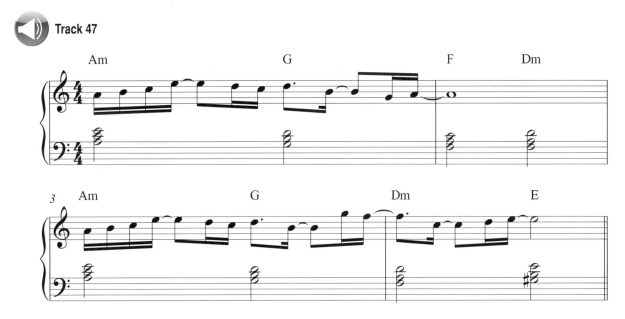

You'll see that we've used left-hand triad inversions to voice lead smoothly from one chord to the next. Again, the chords are landing on the downbeats, even though the melody may be anticipating (for example, during measure 4).

Let's see how the previous 16th-note harmonization guidelines have been applied to this example:

- In measure 1, the melody notes landing on (or anticipating) the downbeats are A, E, D, and B. These notes together aren't contained within any of the diatonic triads in A minor that we saw earlier, which suggests we will at least need a chord rhythm of "two chords per measure" to harmonize the melody. So when dividing the measure in half for harmonization purposes, we see that the melody notes A (on beat 1) and E (anticipating beat 2) are both within the A minor triad, and the melody notes D (on beat 3) and B (anticipating beat 4) are both within the G major triad, resulting in the "two chords per measure" shown here.

- In measure 2, the only melody note to accommodate is A (anticipating beat 1). There are several diatonic triads containing this melody note (Am, F, Dm, etc.). Here, we're maintaining the "two chords per measure" chord rhythm by using F major (on beat 1) followed by D minor (on beat 3). This is a creative preference. We don't *have* to use the same chord rhythm (although in the contemporary styles we may prefer to, in order to maintain harmonic movement and interest).

- Measure 3 is substantially similar to measure 1, for harmonization purposes.

- In measure 4, we'll again need a "two chords per measure" chord rhythm to accommodate the melody notes F (anticipating beat 1) and E (anticipating beat 3), which are not in the same diatonic triad. Although the F major triad (containing both F and C) would have been the obvious choice on beat 1, the D minor triad is subjectively used here for variation and interest (as we've already used the F major triad on beat 1 of measure 2). The melody note F (anticipating beat 1) is within this triad, but the C (anticipating beat 2) is a 7th of this chord (technically upgrading the harmony to a Dm7 chord at this point). This is a safe upgrade in all but the most basic contemporary styles.

Next, we'll develop this harmonization in a more professional-sounding R&B ballad piano style.

Track 48
Backing Track Style: R&B Ballad

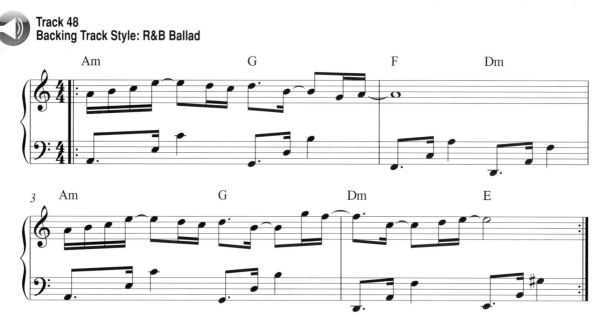

The left-hand part is using open triad arpeggios (as seen earlier in Tracks 16, 24, etc.) except that we're now landing on the last 16th note of beats 1 and 3, instead of halfway through these beats. Technically, this creates a 16th-note pickup into beats 2 and 4 of each measure, resulting in greater "forward motion" into the next downbeat. This is a staple ingredient of R&B ballad piano!

For much more information on R&B ballad piano styles, please see our *Pop Piano Book*, published by Hal Leonard.

Now let's expand the harmonization choices to include the most common four-part chords in the key of A minor. As before, these chords will sound denser and more sophisticated compared to the triads we've used so far in this key.

The most commonly used four-part chord options from the previously shown A minor scales can be summarized as follows:

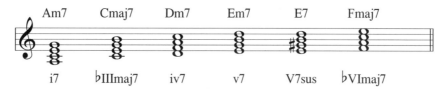

The different A minor scales allow us to derive both the Em7 and E7 chords shown here (suspending the E7 chord, i.e., E7sus, would also be possible).

Next, we'll expand all of the diatonic triad choices used in Tracks 47–48 to their corresponding four-part chords (with the exception of the G major triad, where we'll try the Em7 instead as a *substitute* four-part chord). In contemporary styles, there are no useful four-part versions of the "♭VII" triad in minor (i.e., G major in the key of A minor), which is why we used the Em7 in this example as a substitute (this chord contains all of the notes in the original G major triad). To begin with, we'll play basic root-position, four-part chords in the left hand to accompany the melody in the right hand.

Track 49

As seen earlier, playing root-position, four-part chords in the left hand sounds rather basic. For a more polished result, we can arpeggiate (play in a broken-chord style) these left-hand chords in an R&B ballad style, as follows:

Track 50
Backing Track Style: R&B Ballad

CHAPTER 3
USING UPPER TRIADS AND BASS INVERSIONS

VOICING LARGER CHORDS WITH UPPER TRIADS

So far, we've been choosing either triads or four-part chords to harmonize melodies, and we've started to voice the upper triad of the four-part chords (i.e., the 3rd–5th–7th) in the right hand over the chord root in the left hand.

Next, we'll further develop this upper triad triad technique, to create or imply *five-part* (or larger) chords when harmonizing. We'll start out with the primary triads (I, IV, and V) in the key of C major, and then see which larger chords might use these as upper triads. This is a great way to spice up your contemporary harmonizations and arrangements!

First, we'll review the primary triads in C major, as seen in Chapter 1.

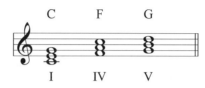

Next, we'll work with a brief melody in C major, using eighth notes with rhythmic anticipations.

 Track 51

If we were to apply primary triad harmonization to this melody (as outlined in Chapter 2), the results could be as follows:

 Track 52

Notice that these left-hand triad inversions are anticipating beat 3 in each measure, together with the melody (unlike earlier examples where the melody anticipated the chord changes). This is a stylistic choice. Anticipating the chord rhythms in this way adds more off-beat urgency, or *syncopation*, to the chord rhythms.

In order to develop this harmonization using upper triads, we need to see which larger chords contain the primary triads (C, F, and G major) in this key. For now, we'll limit ourselves to larger chords which still belong to (are diatonic to) the key of C major, as shown on the next page.

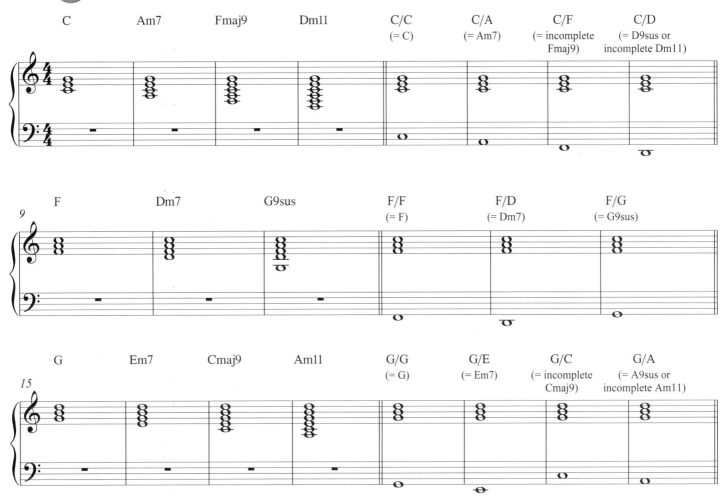

Now let's take a deep breath! Don't worry, it may *look* a little complicated, but it'll actually be simpler to use than you think! Each line of this example relates to one of the primary triads in C (i.e., C, F, or G major).

The first line (measure 1) starts with the C major triad. This is followed by some larger chords that this C major triad "lives in" (i.e., the following Am7, Fmaj9, and Dm11). But, the larger these chords get, the less likely you are to play all of these notes "stacked together" in contemporary styles. Instead, you're more likely to voice them with an upper triad in the right hand (over a root note in the left hand), as seen in measures 4–8 of this line. Just so it's clear, the chord symbol C/C means "C major triad placed over C in the bass," the chord symbol C/A means "C major triad placed over A in the bass," and so on.

Similarly, on the second line, the F major triad occurs within the Dm7 and G9sus chords, and on the third line, the G major triad occurs within the Em7, Cmaj9, and Am11 chords.

The bottom line is this: As an alternative to harmonizing a melody note or phrase with a simple primary triad, we can try using one of the larger chords which that triad belongs to and then voice that chord using an upper structure from the right-hand side of Track 53. Let's try this technique on the previous melody fragment from Tracks 51–52 (now with a pop/rock rhythm section).

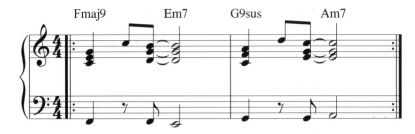

The right-hand triads are now inverted below the melody (similar to earlier examples in Tracks 33, 41, etc.) except these triads are now upper structures of larger chords, as shown on the right-hand side of Track 53.

We can compare this example to the earlier harmonization of the same melody in Track 52.

- On beat 1 of measure 1, the C major triad is now placed over the root of F (see Track 53, measure 7) creating a voicing for an Fmaj9 chord (technically incomplete as the 3rd of the chord, A, is not included).

- Anticipating beat 3 of measure 1, the G major triad is now placed over the root of E (see Track 53, measure 20) creating a voicing for an Em7 chord.

- On beat 1 of measure 2, the F major triad is now placed over the root of G (see Track 53, measure 14) creating a voicing for a G9sus chord (although the 5th of the chord is not included here).

- Anticipating beat 3 of measure 2, the C major triad is now placed over the root of A (see Track 53, measure 6), creating a voicing for an Am7 chord.

You can hear that this all creates a more interesting and sophisticated sound than the simple triads we used to harmonize this melody in Track 52. So while we wouldn't do this in very basic or traditional styles, these options are often used in contemporary pop/R&B styles.

One more thing about the piano styling in Track 54: While the right-hand triads are anticipating beat 3 (per the melody rhythm), the left hand is now landing on beat 3, so we're back to the right hand anticipating the left hand as in earlier examples. Also, the left hand is adding an eighth-note pickup right before beat 3, which happens to coincide with the right-hand anticipations. This is deliberate, but it may sound odd at first if you're new to pop/rock piano styles!

For much more information on using upper triad voicings, please see our *Pop Piano Book* and *Contemporary Music Theory Level Two* book. Both books are published by Hal Leonard. Have fun experimenting with these upper triad harmonization options!

APPLYING BASS INVERSIONS TO TRIADS

Let's take a look at the next melody to harmonize, again in the key of C major. This time, we'll use 16th-note subdivisions and anticipations.

 Track 55

If we were to apply primary triad (I, IV, or V) harmonization to this melody, we would most likely need two chords per measure (per the harmonization rules developed in Chapter 1), as follows:

Note the left-hand triad inversions are landing on beats 1 and 3 (together with the melody). This time, the melody is anticipating beats 2 and 4 of measure 1 and beat 2 of measure 2 (by 16th notes), but is *not* anticipating beats 1 or 3 (unlike the earlier 16th-note melody example in Tracks 46–50).

Now to help kick this harmonization up a notch, we'll develop the concept of *bass inversions*. Bass inversions occur when we invert (or place) a triad over its own 3rd or 5th in the bass. For example, the chord symbol C/E means "C major triad inverted over its 3rd (E) in the bass." These voicings are different to the upper triads seen in Tracks 53–54 in that we have taken a note which is already in the upper triad (i.e., the 3rd or the 5th) and used it in the left-hand bass part.

Let's take a quick look at the primary triads in C major and the different ways we can place them over their 3rds or 5ths in the bass.

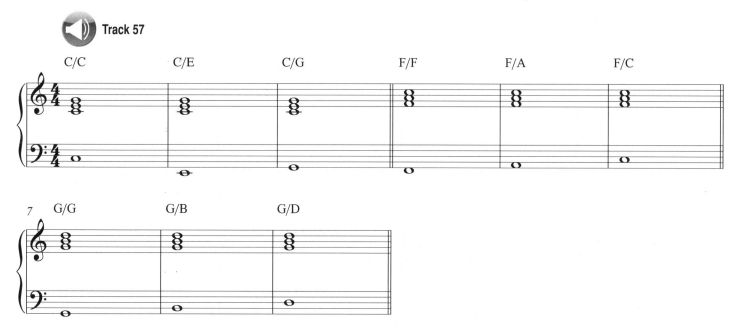

In measure 1, we've started with a basic C/C voicing (as shown in Track 53, measure 5), which is a simple voicing for a C major chord. But then in measure 2, the C major triad has been inverted over its own 3rd in the bass, resulting in the C/E voicing shown. Then in measure 3, the C major triad has been inverted over its own 5th in the bass, resulting in the C/G voicing shown. Similarly, bass inversion voicings are shown for the F major triad in measures 5–6 and for the G major triad in measures 8–9.

Now let's return to the melody from Track 55 and harmonize with a combination of upper triads (from Track 53, right-hand side) and bass inversions (from Track 57), played in a rock ballad style.

Now the triads from the left-hand part in Track 56 are inverted below the melody in the right hand (similar to Track 54 and earlier examples). These triads are either upper structures of larger chords, or bass inversion voicings, as explained below.

- On beat 1 of measure 1, the C major triad is now placed over the root of A (see Track 53, measure 6), creating a voicing for an Am7 chord.

- On beat 3 of measure 1, the F major triad (now "split" between the left and right hands) is placed over the root of D (see Track 53, measure 13), creating a voicing for a Dm7 chord.

- On beat 1 of measure 2, the C major triad is now placed over its own 3rd (E, the lowest note in the left-hand part - see Track 57, measure 2), resulting in a C/E chord voicing.

- On beat 3 of measure 2, the G major triad is now placed over its own 3rd (B, the lowest note in the left-hand part—see Track 57, measure 8), resulting in a G/B chord voicing.

Note that we now have two-note intervals in the left-hand part, instead of just the single-note roots seen in earlier examples.

- In measure 1, we have a "root–7th" interval in the left hand, on the Am7 and Dm7 chords. This is a staple left-hand voicing in jazz, blues, and more evolved pop styles.

- In measure 3, we have a "3rd–root" interval in the left hand, on the C/E and G/B chords. This is a nice thickening of the voicing texture for a major chord inverted over its own 3rd, if space permits.

There are many harmonization options available when including upper structures and bass inversions in the mix. As always, you are encouraged to experiment!

HARMONIZING PENTATONIC SCALE MELODIES

The next melody example uses the notes in an A *pentatonic* scale. Let's take a moment to review how the pentatonic scale (sometimes referred to as the *major pentatonic* scale) is derived.

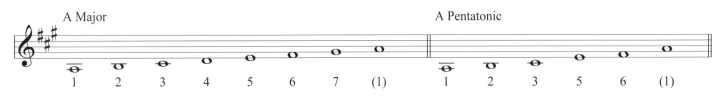

On the left in this example, we see the A major scale (together with the A major key signature). On the right, we see the A pentatonic scale, derived by removing the 4th and 7th degrees from A major.

You may remember that back in Chapter 1, we labelled the 4th and 7th degrees of a major scale as "Fa" and Ti," respectively (using solfege syllables), and that these active tones often resolve to adjacent resting tones in melodies. Well, when we eliminate these active tones from the major scale (thereby creating the pentatonic scale), we reduce the "leading" or resolving tendency in melodies which use this scale. Consequently, pentatonic scale melodies are more easily able to float over different harmonies and progressions, as we will shortly see.

Let's move on to the next melody example, using an A pentatonic scale.

Track 59

We see that this melody repeats the same one-measure phrase throughout and uses eighth-note subdivisions and anticipations (the melody note A landing on the "&" of beat 2 in each measure, is anticipating beat 3). Bearing in mind our earlier rules for eighth-note melodies (looking for melody notes on primary beats or their anticipations when harmonizing), we see that the note A is the most prominent or significant melody note in this example, therefore any useful harmonization would need to take this into account.

We'll start out with a very basic harmonization, using an A major chord throughout.

Track 60

Again, we've used inverted triads below the melody in the right hand, above the chord roots played in the left hand.

Just staying on the A major chord here is rather static and not particularly interesting! The melody note of A falls on all of the primary beats (1 and 3) or their anticipations, and the A major triad contains this note for the simplest solution in the harmony. Note that the melodic *passing tones* in between (i.e., the E and F♯ in each measure) also work with the A major chord. This frequently occurs with pentatonic melodies. The melody notes "in between" the changes will often work with the harmonization that is being used.

Next, we'll vary the harmony with a "one chord per measure" chord rhythm, moving between the I chord (A major) and the IV chord (D major). Moving back and forth between the I and IV major chords in this way is typical in more basic rock and country music styles.

Track 61

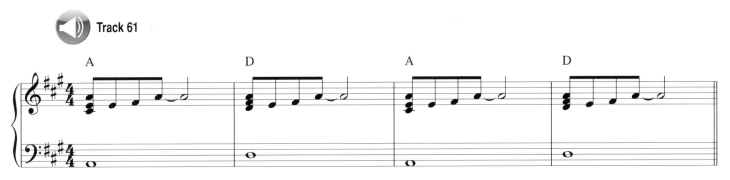

We know that this is a repetitive melody with the note A on all of the primary beats (or anticipations), but we can still choose to change chords according to a desired chord rhythm (one chord per measure here) as long as they fit with the melody. The melody note A is the root of the I chord (A major) and the 5th of the IV chord (D major), so we could alternate between these chords as shown above. Note that the melodic passing tones of E and F♯ work with both the A major and D major chords used. Technically, the resulting chord functions are as follows:

- In measures 1 and 3, the E and F♯ are the 5th and 6th of the A major chord, respectively.

- In measures 2 and 4, the E and F♯ are the 9th and 3rd of the D major chord, respectively.

Our next treatment of this melody builds on the last version, with the previous A and D major triads now as upper triads of larger chords, using the possibilities shown in Track 53 (now transposed to the key of A major).

Track 62

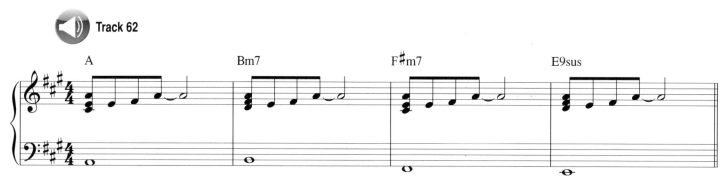

We can analyze the harmonization used in this example as follows:

- In measure 1, the A major triad is still placed over the root of A (as previously shown in Tracks 60 and 61).

- In measure 2, the D major triad is placed over the root of B, creating a voicing for a Bm7 chord (same as in Track 53 measure 13, but transposed to A major).

- In measure 3, the A major triad is placed over the root of F♯, creating a voicing for an F♯m7 chord (same as in Track 53 measure 6, again transposed to A major).

- In measure 4, the D major triad is placed over the root of E, creating a voicing for an E9sus chord (same as in Track 53 measure 14, again transposed to A major).

You can hear that using upper triad harmonization in this way, creates a more sophisticated sound (compared to Track 61 for example), which is often suitable for more contemporary pop/rock or smooth jazz styles. Again, this harmonization is not necessarily *better*, it's just *different*. These treatments have different stylistic implications, which you should bear in mind when harmonizing! As before, there are various choices available when using upper triad harmonization. Feel free to experiment (and refer back to Track 53 as necessary).

Now we'll take this latest harmonization, and stylize it in a modern pop piano style, as follows:

Track 63
Backing Track Style: Modern Pop

In the piano part, note that the right-hand part is the same as for Track 62 (inverted triads below melody), but the left-hand part has more movement: either root–5th–root (in measures 1 and 4), or root–5th–7th (in measures 2 and 3). Rhythmically, the left hand is anticipating beat 3 in each measure together with the right hand (this is quite common in modern rock styles).

Our next melody example uses an F minor pentatonic scale in the key of F minor. We'll need to work through a couple of theory steps beforehand to understand how the minor pentatonic scale is created.

First, we'll review the notes in an A♭ major scale as follows:

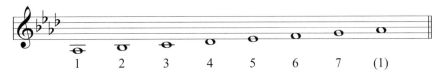

To get from this A♭ major scale to an F minor pentatonic scale, we'll need to do the following:

- Remove the 4th and 7th degrees from this A♭ major scale (in this case D♭ and G), creating an A♭ pentatonic scale (similar to what we did with the A major scale, earlier in this chapter).

- Then, displace the A♭ pentatonic scale to start on its relative minor, which is the note F.

These steps are shown below.

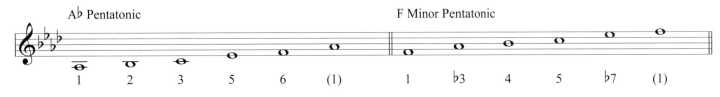

In the first measure we see the A♭ pentatonic scale, derived as above. If we then displace this scale (containing A♭, B♭, C, E♭, and F) to start on the note F, we get the F minor pentatonic scale (containing F, A♭, B♭, C, and E♭) as shown in the second measure.

Just a quick theory reminder: We saw back in Chapter 1 that the relative minor key was built from the 6th degree of the corresponding major key. So as F is the 6th degree of A♭ major, we can say that the keys of A♭ major and F minor are relative to one another and share the same key signature.

For more information on minor scales, keys, and key signatures, please see our *Contemporary Music Theory Level One* book. Detailed information on pentatonic and minor pentatonic scales can be found in our *Contemporary Music Theory Level Two* book. Both are published by Hal Leonard.

Let's move on to the next melody example, which uses the F minor pentatonic scale.

Track 64

You can see that all of these melody notes are within an F minor pentatonic scale, and the melody note F is repeated on beat 1 of each measure (and also occurs later in measures 1, 3, and 4). All of this (together with the key signature) suggests that we are in the key of F minor overall.

We see that this melody uses two similar two-measure phrases, this time with 16th-note subdivisions and anticipations. For example, the melody note E♭ landing on the last 16th note of beat 2 (or the "a" of beat 2) in measures 1–3, is anticipating beat 3 by a 16th note. (Refer back to Track 45 and accompanying text if you need to remind yourself of this.)

Because this melody is limited to the F minor pentatonic scale, we would expect it to be able to float over different harmonies available in the key of F minor (similar to our discussions regarding the earlier melody in A pentatonic, in Tracks 60–62). Let's first take a look at the commonly used diatonic triads in the key of F minor.

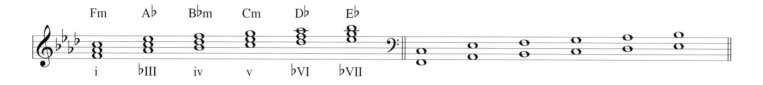

In the left-hand measure we see the most commonly used diatonic triad options in the key of F minor, for harmonizing "minor pentatonic" melodies. In the right-hand measure, we see corresponding "root–5th," left-hand voicings for each of these chords. These left-hand 5th intervals are powerful, open-sounding, and are useful in rock and funk styles. When used to support minor pentatonic melodies in the right hand, they will frequently allow different chords to be used for the same melody note or motif, without harmonic conflicts occurring. More about this shortly!

Meanwhile, let's start with a very simple harmonization of the melody in Track 64, by using an F minor triad (i.e., the i, or tonic chord, in the key of F minor) throughout.

Track 65

Note that here, we've simply inverted an F minor triad below the melody in the right hand (on beat 1 of each measure) and played the root of F in the left hand. While this harmonization certainly works, again, it's rather static, and we would normally prefer to have more movement and variation.

So next, we'll apply a "one chord per measure" harmonic rhythm, using some of the left-hand, 5th-interval voicings for the common diatonic triads in this key. Rather than look for the melody notes on primary beats which are within diatonic triads, we can instead select from these chords somewhat *independently of the melody*, knowing that the melody notes from the minor pentatonic scale will likely not conflict with the harmony (particularly if we're using the less definitive, root–5th voicings in the left hand).

Using this approach, below is one of various chord progressions we could apply to this melody.

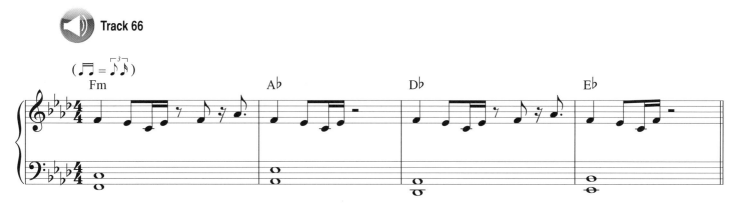

We can analyze how this harmonization relates to the melody, as follows:

- In measure 1, the prominent melody note of F is the *root* of the F minor chord. The other melody notes (E♭, C, and A♭) in this measure are the 7th, 5th, and 3rd of this chord, respectively, and they technically imply an Fm7 chord in total. This is perfectly OK on a tonic chord in minor, even in simpler contemporary styles.

- In measure 2, the melody note of F is now the 6th of the A♭ major chord. The 6th is an available *extension* on the major chord (if we extend it beyond a triad). Having a chord extension in the melody on beat 1 creates a more sophisticated sound (compared to just having either the root, 3rd, or 5th in the melody). However, we are repeating some of the melodic phrase from the first measure, which has already been harmonized with the tonic chord of the key in that measure. So by the second measure, we've already defined the key of F minor key to our ear, and are more likely to "get away with" the chord extension (6th) in the melody on the following chord. The other melody notes (E♭ and C) in this measure are the 5th and 3rd of this chord, respectively— the basic chord tones of the A♭ major chord.

- In measure 3, the melody note of F is now the 3rd of the D♭ major chord. The other melody notes (E♭, C, and A♭) in this measure are the 9th, 7th, and 5th of this chord respectively, technically implying a D♭maj9 chord in total. Although we have a basic chord tone (the 3rd) in the melody on beat 1, the chord extensions later in the measure (i.e., the 7th and 9th) do create a more sophisticated sound on this major chord.

- In measure 4, the melody note of F is now the 9th of the E♭ major chord (another available extension on this chord). As before, having a chord extension in the melody on beat 1 creates a more sophisticated sound. However, for similar reasons as explained for measure 2, this is likely to work in the context of the key of F minor, which has already been defined. The other melody notes (E♭ and C) in this measure are the root and 6th of this chord, respectively. Again, the 6th is an available extension on the major chord, as seen in measure 2.

The bottom line is this: In the contemporary styles, we can get away with the more sophisticated harmonizations on beat 1 of measures 2 and 4 (i.e., the melody being the 6th and the 9th of two different major chords), as we've already established the minor key and the melodic motif beforehand. In other contexts (i.e., using such chords in an opening measure), these harmonizations may be too sophisticated for many pop music applications.

In the example on the next page, we'll develop the piano styling of this harmonization, in a swing-16ths funk style (sometimes referred to as a *funk shuffle*).

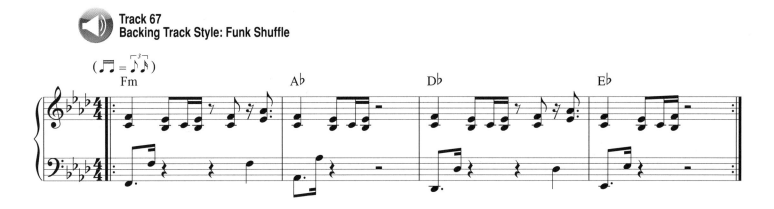

Note that some piano techniques that are idiomatic to R&B/funk styles have been used here, such as:

- In the right hand, where *perfect 4th* intervals have been added below the melody within the F minor pentatonic scale restrictions. This gives a transparent, hollow sound and is a staple funk keyboard technique.

- In the left hand, further root notes have been added in a "rhythmic conversation" with the right-hand part (apart from both hands landing on beat 1 of each measure).

For much more information on R&B/funk comping styles, please see our *Pop Piano Book* published by Hal Leonard.

Now it's time to look at another harmonization of the F minor pentatonic scale melody from Track 64.

Earlier, we showed the common diatonic triads used to harmonize F minor pentatonic melodies (Fm, A♭, B♭m, Cm, D♭, and E♭). As mentioned in the text following Track 65, these chords are largely interchangeable when harmonizing this type of melody. Next, we'll apply a different chord progression (from these options) to the same melody in the key of F minor, again using root–5th voicings in the left hand.

Track 68

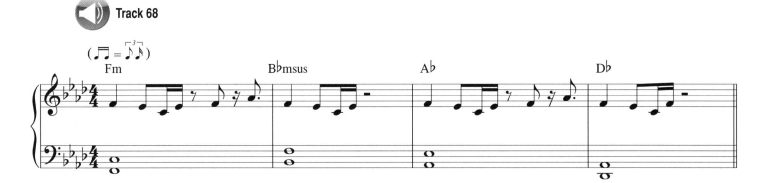

We can analyze how this harmonization relates to the melody, as follows:

- Measure 1: The same comments as for measure 1 in Track 66.

- Measure 2: The melody note of F is now the 5th of the B♭ minor chord, and the following melody notes E♭ and C are the 4th and 9th of the chord, respectively. However, the 4th gives this chord a suspended quality, as the definitive 3rd of the chord (which would have been D♭) is *not* present. This is why the chord symbol "B♭msus" has been shown here for your information. However, we would still often just see "B♭m" written in a chart or fake book in this type of situation.

- Measure 3: same comments as for measure 2 in Track 66.

- Measure 4: same comments as for measure 3 in Track 66.

Again, we can stylize this harmonization in a *swing-16ths* funk piano style, such as the one below.

Refer back to the text following Track 67 for some information on the R&B/funk piano techniques used in this example!

CHAPTER 4
CHROMATIC AND MODAL MELODIES

CHROMATIC MELODY BASICS

So far, we've been harmonizing melodies which belong to a major or minor key, and for some minor key melodies, we've needed to contradict the key signature with flat or natural signs, depending on the minor scale(s) used in the melody (see "Minor Scales and Keys" in Chapter 2).

Additionally, there are a number of other reasons why we may encounter *accidentals* (sharp, flat, or natural signs) in the melody we're trying to harmonize. Generally, we can say that melodies which move outside of a key restriction can be termed *chromatic* (the opposite of diatonic).

A complete treatment of chromatic melody and harmony is beyond the scope of this book, but here are some principles to get you started with harmonizing chromatic melodies.

When you see accidentals contradicting the key signature in contemporary melodies, most often one of the following situations is occurring:

1. The melody is using different minor scales within a minor key (as mentioned above).

2. The music is changing key, either momentarily (for a certain number of measures) or for the remainder of the piece. In this case, the harmony needs to reflect the new key that is implied by the melody.

3. The music is *modal*, meaning the melody and harmonization is still diatonic to a major scale, but that scale has been displaced to start on a different tonic. More about this shortly!

4. The music is combining two scales or modes together within a key, for example the C major and C natural minor scales (which can be referred to as a *major/minor mix*). Again, more on this shortly!

5. The music is not adhering to any particular key restriction (common in some contemporary jazz styles). In this case, we'll often make use of *parallel motion* harmonization, an idea we'll talk about in Chapter 5.

Momentary Key Changes

When a diatonic scale degree is sharped or flatted, this is typically a sign that the music is changing key (situation 2 above). Often, this can be referred to as a *momentary* key change. More sophisticated music styles (especially jazz) routinely make use of momentary key changes in the harmony. We'll explore this more with the next two examples.

First, we'll look at an example where a diatonic scale degree has been sharped. This chromatic note will then often become the 7th degree (solfege syllable "Ti") of a new key and can then be harmonized with the V chord of that key.

A good example of this situation occurs in the famous song, "Abide with Me." Most of the eight-measure excerpt on the next page is harmonized with diatonic triads in C major, but towards the end the melody note F is raised to F♯, implying the 7th degree of G major.

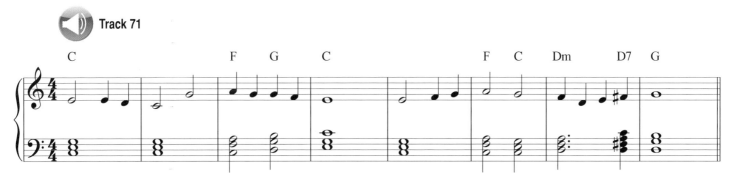

Again, we're using basic triads in the left hand below the melody, inverted to voice lead smoothly from left to right, as shown in earlier examples.

In the first six measures, we're applying primary triad harmonization techniques from Chapter 1, using either one or two chords per measure. Then, in measure 7, we have the melody notes F and D on beats 1 and 2, respectively, suggesting the ii triad (Dm) as a good option to start with.

However, on beat 4 in measure 7, we have the chromatic note of F♯ in the melody, which resolves up to G in the next measure. This suggests a "Ti–Do" (7th degree to 1st degree) movement in the key of G that can most basically be harmonized with a D major triad, which is the V chord in the key of G. You may like to review Track 1 for the "Ti–Do" melodic movement in the key of C if needed.

Although it's not very common to place chord changes on beats 2 or 4 in contemporary 4/4 styles (particularly with this simple melodic rhythm), here it's recommended because the chromatic melody note F♯ falls on beat 4 of the measure. Be on the lookout for this type of situation when harmonizing!

As an alternative to strengthen the implied V–I chord movement in the key of G, we could "upgrade" the D major triad to a D dominant 7th chord, as follows:

Track 71

This example is the same as Track 70, except that we now have a D7 (dominant) chord harmonizing the chromatic note of F♯ on beat 4 of measure 7. This makes the V chord lead more strongly back to the I or tonic chord and is suitable in this more traditional style.

Next, we'll look at a melody example where a diatonic scale degree has been lowered. This chromatic note will often become the 4th degree (solfege syllable "Fa") of a new key and can then be harmonized with the IV chord of that key, among other options that we will develop.

Track 72

Following previous rules, we could again harmonize the first measure with a C major triad. (The melody notes C and G on primary beats or their anticipations are within this C major triad.) But in the second measure, we have a B♭ in the melody on beat 1. This is a flatted scale degree, so we can try treating this as the 4th degree of a new key (F major in this case).

We could then harmonize this melody note of B♭ with the IV chord of the new key (B♭ major), which could then lead back to the I chord of this key (F major) to harmonize the melody note A in the third measure. Next, we'll develop this harmonization in a pop ballad piano style.

Track 73
Backing Track Style: Pop Ballad

Here, the left hand is playing a sparser version of the open triad arpeggio pattern used in earlier examples (see Tracks 16, 24, etc.), now landing on the last eighth-note of beat 2 of each measure, adding more forward motion into beat 3.

As an alternative, try harmonizing the B♭ in measure 2 of this melody with a V chord in the key of F. We saw two forms of the four-part V chord in F, back in Chapter 2, the C7 and C7sus chords, both of which have the note B♭ as their 7th and could therefore be used to harmonize this measure. Just to review, these are dominant 7th and suspended dominant 7th chords, respectively. Either of these chords will lead well to the F major chord on a V–I basis (especially the more traditional C7 form). Now we'll amend the previous pop ballad piano styling to include the C7 dominant 7th chord, as follows:

Track 74
Backing Track Style: Pop Ballad

Looking at the second measure in the left-hand part, we now have a "root–7th–3rd" arpeggio pattern (similar to the "root–5th–3rd" open triad arpeggio pattern on the C major chord in the first measure, but now adding the 7th of the chord). Here, the 7th and 3rd of the C7 chord are critical tones which help define the dominant chord to our ear and help the chord "lead" to the following F major chord.

Now we'll vary this harmonization by using a suspended dominant 7th (C7sus).

Track 75
Backing Track Style: Pop Ballad

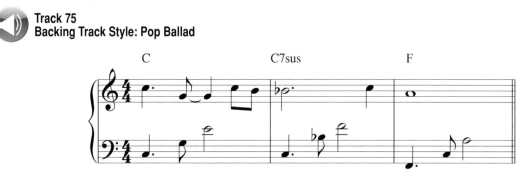

Comparing the second measure here to the corresponding measure in Track 74: In the left-hand pattern, we've replaced the 3rd of the chord (E) with the suspended 4th (F), which creates a smoother and more pop-friendly sound on this V chord (see earlier comments on the C7sus chord in Track 41).

This is only a brief introduction to the concept of momentary keys and key changes when harmonizing, but it should be enough to get you started. Have fun!

For much more information on momentary keys and key changes used in jazz styles, please refer to *Contemporary Music Theory Level Two*, published by Hal Leonard.

MIXOLYDIAN MELODY HARMONIZATION

Next, we'll take a look at a modal melody. When a melody is derived from a different major scale than the key signature indicates, this is typically a sign that the music is using a modal scale. (This is situation 3 described at the beginning of this chapter.) For modal melodies, the tonic, or "home base," of the melody is normally indicated by the key signature.

A modal scale can be thought of as a displaced version of a major scale. A theory term we need to get comfortable with here is the *relative major scale*, which is the scale that has been displaced to create the mode being used. Let's demonstrate these concepts by looking at how an F major scale can be displaced to create the C *Mixolydian* mode.

Here's a reminder of the notes in a F major scale:

Now if we take these notes and reposition them to start on the note C, we get a C Mixolydian mode.

We could also get the same result by taking a C major scale, and lowering (or flatting) the 7th degree by a half step (i.e., B to Bb).

Here's some more theory so we can really enjoy the fun stuff:

- The term *Mixolydian* here in practice means "any given major scale starting on its 5th degree." So if we know (or can figure out) that C is the 5th degree of an F major scale, then all we need to do is start an F major scale on the note C to derive a C Mixolydian mode. This is an important point which I often reinforce in piano and improv classes.

- The relative major scale of C Mixolydian is F major. This is the scale which has been displaced to create the mode.

- There are various other modes (displacements of major scales) in common usage, including Dorian, Lydian, and so on. We don't have space to go into them all here, but for much more information on modal scales and their relative major scales, please see our *Contemporary Music Theory Level One* book, published by Hal Leonard.

So why is all this significant when we're harmonizing melodies? Well, we'll want to know if the melody we're trying to harmonize is modal in order to then use this knowledge to access appropriate chord choices. With this in mind, let's look at a modal melody using a Mixolydian mode.

Note that as this melody is repeated, we hear the note C as the tonic, which is why we've used the key signature of C major here (no sharps and no flats). However, we also see that the melody note of B♭ (rather than B) is used throughout. This means that we are actually using the F major scale in the melody but displaced so that the note C is the new tonic. This melody is therefore using the C Mixolydian mode as described above. Mixolydian melodies are a commonly used device in pop styles, with Glenn Frey's "The Heat Is On" and Gary Numan's "Cars" being two famous examples.

So to harmonize this melody (even though C is the "tonic"), we can use the diatonic chords from F major derived earlier in Chapter 2. In this case, it's typical to start the modal harmonization with a strong I or tonic chord (C major in this case, to establish the tonic of the mode), as shown in a modern rock style in the following example:

All of the triad choices in this example are diatonic to F major, and can be derived using earlier guidelines for diatonic triad harmonization of the melody. But the C major chord used for the first measure sounds like the tonic or I chord, particularly when this four-measure phrase is repeated on the audio track. The rock band Coldplay used this Mixolydian triad concept when harmonizing famous songs such as "Clocks" and "Speed of Sound."

Note the piano styling here which is in a more modern rock style. Some of the triads are split between the left and right hands, and the left hand is playing arpeggios in measures 2 and 4, continuing the syncopated rhythm established in the melody.

This is just an introduction to the many possibilities available within the Mixolydian mode (and modal harmony in general). As usual, you are encouraged to experiment!

MAJOR/MINOR MIX MELODY HARMONIZATION

Finally, we'll take a look at a melody which uses both the major scale and natural minor scale (built from the same tonic (i.e., C major and C natural minor together). I refer to this situation as a *major/minor mix* in my books and classes. Again, this is quite common across a range of contemporary melodic styles. So with the note C as the tonic or "home base," the total possibilities available within these scales would be as shown on the next page.

C Major

C Natural Minor

OK, so we need a little more "modal" theory here before we proceed. The C natural minor scale shown above, is also a displaced version of an E♭ major scale. We could therefore call it a C *Aeolian* mode, as *Aeolian* in practice means, "any given major scale starting from its 6th degree," and C is the 6th degree of an E♭ major scale.

This is important here because the diatonic triads we might use in the key of E♭ might also be used to harmonize these melody notes within the C natural minor scale. These could then be combined with diatonic triads in C major, leading to the following combined set of harmonization options in C major/minor mix.

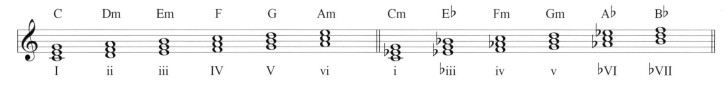

Again, we've just included the most commonly used diatonic triads here, from both the major scale and the natural minor scale.

Next, we'll look at a melody which uses both the C major and C natural minor scales, as follows:

Track 78

Note the key signature used here has no sharps and no flats, corresponding to the major key (i.e., C major). We see that this melody includes the notes E, A, and B from the C major scale, as well as E♭, A♭, and B♭ from the C natural minor scale. The overall tonic is still heard as C, even though we are combining melody notes from these two scales.

Using the previous diatonic triads from both the C major and C natural minor scales, and applying either one or two chords per measure, one of various harmonization options for this melody is shown below.

Track 79
Backing Track Style: Pop/Rock

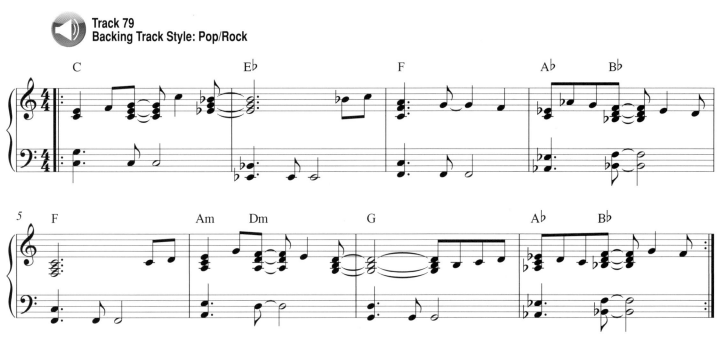

The piano part uses triads below the melody in the right hand, together with root–5th intervals and eighth-note pickups in the left, for a driving pop/rock rhythmic feel.

Let's look at this triad harmonization more closely.

- In measure 1, the melody notes landing on (or anticipating) the primary beats 1 and 3 are E and G. These are within the I chord (C major), a good choice to help establish the tonic key at the beginning of the phrase.

- In measure 2, the melody note B♭ anticipates beat 1 (and is repeated on beat 4). Various triads from C natural minor contain B♭, including the ♭III (E♭ major) used here.

- In measure 3, the melody notes A, G, and F land on beat 1, the "&" of beat 2 (anticipating beat 3), and beat 4, respectively, suggesting this measure be harmonized from the chords in C major. Here, we chose just one chord for this measure, the IV, F major triad (D minor would also have been an option). Although the melody note G that anticipates beat 3 is not within the F major triad, it's an available upper extension (9th) on the chord. We could instead have used a "two chords per measure" harmonic rhythm if we wanted this melody note to be a more basic tone of a chord. Again, this is a creative choice.

- In measure 4, the melody notes landing on (or anticipating) the primary beats are E♭ and F. Here, we've chosen two chords for this measure (A♭ and B♭) to add movement and interest. The melody notes are the 5ths of each of these chords, respectively.

- In measure 5, the melody note C lands on beat 1 (and is repeated on beat 4). Various available triads contain the melody note C, including the "IV" F major used here (which gives us a useful *circle-of-4ths*, or implied IV–I bass movement, from the preceding B♭ chord).

- In measure 6, the melody notes landing on (or anticipating) the primary beats are E and F. Here, we've again chosen two chords for this measure (Am and Dm) for more movement. The melody notes are the 5th and 3rd of each of these chords, respectively.

- In measure 7, the melody note D anticipates beat 1 (and is repeated later in the measure). Various available triads contain the melody note D, including the "V" G major used here (which gives us a useful circle of 5ths or implied V–I bass movement from the preceding Dm chord).

- Measure 8: similar comments as measure 4.

Next, we'll apply a different harmonization to this melody, this time using some of the upper triad and bass inversion voicings developed in the last chapter (see Tracks 53 and 57).

In the right hand of the piano part, we've used either the I, IV or V major triads (C, F, or G, from the C major scale), or the ♭III, ♭VI, or ♭VII major triads (E♭, A♭, or B♭, from the C natural minor scale). Then, each of the triads chosen has been further treated in one of the following ways:

- Built from the 3rd of a minor 7th chord (see Track 53, measures 6, 13, and 20).

- Built from the 5th of an implied major 9th chord (see Track 53, measures 7 and 21).

- Built from the 7th of a suspended dominant 9th chord (see Track 53, measures 8, 14, and 22).

- Inverted over its own 3rd (see Track 57, measures 2, 5, and 8).

All the resulting voicings are still diatonic to either the C major or C natural minor scales, played in a pop ballad style, as follows:

Track 80
Backing Track Style: Pop/Rock

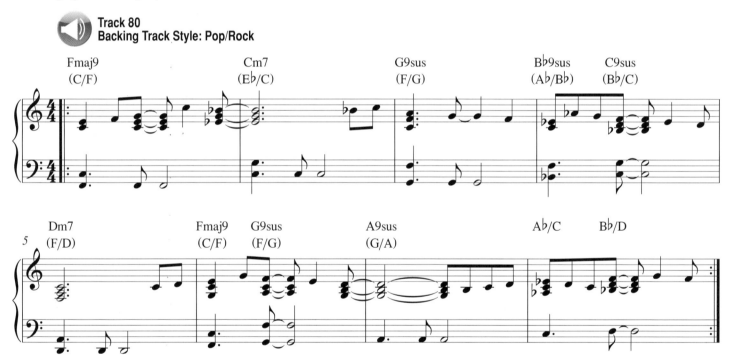

You'll see that for measures 1–7 of this example, two chord symbols are shown for each harmonization choice. The first line contains the composite chord symbols. These consist of a chord root (i.e., "F") followed by a suffix (i.e., "maj9"). The second line shows the corresponding slash chord symbols, showing an upper triad (to the left of the slash) over a root note (to the right of the slash). When reading a chart or fake book, we'll see most often composite symbols, although slash chord symbols for some types of chord (for example, the suspended dominants in measures 3 and 7) are also commonly used.

In measure 8, you'll see that we only have slash chord symbols: A♭/C and B♭/D. These are bass inversion voicings (see explanation on the next page) for which there are no useful or commonly used composite symbol equivalents.

Now we'll look at this upper triad harmonization in more detail (and compare it to the more basic harmonization used in Track 79) as follows:

- In measure 1, the C major triad used in the first measure of Track 79 is now built from the 5th of an implied Fmaj9 chord by placing the triad over the root of F (see Track 53, measure 7). We also saw this harmonization used in the first measure of Track 54.

- In measure 2, the E♭ major triad used in the second measure of Track 79 is now built from the 3rd of a Cm7 chord by placing the triad over the root of C (see similar voicings in measures 6, 13, and 20 of Track 53 for other minor 7th chords).

- In measure 3, the F major triad used in the third measure of Track 79 is now built from the 7th of a G9sus chord by placing the triad over the root of G (see Track 53, measure 14). We also saw this harmonization used in the second measure of Track 54.

- In measure 4, the A♭ and B♭ major triads used in the fourth measure of Track 79 are now built from the 7th of the B♭9sus and C9sus chords, respectively, by placing these triads over the roots of B♭ and C (see similar voicings in measures 8, 14, and 22 of Track 53 for other suspended dominant 9th chords).

- In measure 5, the F major triad used in the fifth measure of Track 79 is now built from the 3rd of a Dm7 chord by placing the triad over the root of D (see Track 53, measure 13).

In measure 6, we see a variation in the right-hand triads. Instead of the A minor and D minor triads from Track 79, we've now used the primary triads of C and F major to harmonize the melody (which gives us more upper triad voicing options). In this measure, we then treat these C and F major triads as follows:

- On beat 1, the C major triad is again built from the 5th of an implied Fmaj9 chord (see measure 1 comments).

- Anticipating beat 3, the F major triad is again built from the 7th of a G9sus chord (see measure 3 comments).

Continuing our analysis for the remainder of Track 80:

- In measure 7, the G major triad used in the 7th measure of Track 79 is now built from the 7th of an A9sus chord by placing the triad over the root of A (see Track 53, measure 22).

- In measure 8, the A♭ and B♭ major triads used in the eighth measure of Track 79 are now inverted or placed over their own 3rds, to create the A♭/C and B♭/D voicings, respectively. (See similar voicings in measures 2, 5, and 8 of Track 57, for other major chords inverted over their own 3rds.)

As you can imagine, there are a lot of possibilities here when we factor in the upper triad harmonization techniques. These sounds are suitable for more evolved pop/R&B styles, as well as today's contemporary and smooth jazz.

CHAPTER 5

MORE ADVANCED HARMONIZATION TOOLS

HARMONIZATION BY BASS LINE

Now it's time to look at a different approach to melody harmonization, which can be termed *harmonization by bass line*. In this approach, we first create a bass line below the melody, then we derive the chord symbols based on the harmonic *implication* of the bass line together with the melody.

In contemporary styles, bass lines created below the melody normally have the following characteristics:

1. Bass lines will often follow the chord rhythms we've seen in earlier examples. This means there will be either one or two bass notes per measure (normally on beats 1 and 3 in 4/4 time).

2. Bass lines will normally move in a linear (*scale-wise*) manner, either ascending or descending. Particularly common in contemporary styles are descending lines beginning on the tonic of the key, characterized as either diatonic (within a major or natural minor scale) or chromatic (by successive half steps).

3. When choosing bass notes to go with the melody, the interval created (i.e., between the bass note and the melody note) will normally be *consonant*, such as 3rds, 4ths, 5ths, or 6ths, or these intervals plus one or more octaves.

With these principles in mind, we'll now take a look at a melody in the key of D major, as follows:

🔊 **Track 81**

Now let's try to find a bass line that will work with this melody. We could start with the tonic of the key (i.e., D) and then descend within a D major scale every two beats. Then, we can see if useful intervals are created between the melody and the bass line, as follows:

🔊 **Track 82**

In this case, all of the intervals created between the melody and the bass line are consonant, with most being 3rds or 6ths, which are harmonically useful as we will see.

The next step is to go through each of these interval relationships and determine which diatonic chords (in D major) they might imply. In particular, we'll need to include *bass inversions* (triads inverted over their own 3rds or 5ths) as these are often the harmonic consequence of using this type of bass line below the melody. First, let's review the most commonly used diatonic triads in the key of D major, shown on the next page.

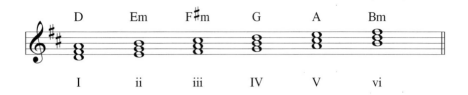

With the above triads (and their bass inversions) available, we can further analyze the harmonic implications of Track 82 as follows:

- In measure 1 on beat 1, the bass and melody notes of D and F♯ form two-thirds of a D major triad (which is a good choice here to begin the harmonization in this key).

- In measure 1 on beat 3, the bass and melody notes of C♯ and A form two-thirds of both the A major and F♯ minor triads. We could use either of these triads, inverted over C♯ in the bass (i.e., either A/C♯ or F♯m/C♯). Here, the A/C♯ sounds stronger and gives more movement from the likely D major triad choice beforehand. In addition, the melody note E on beat 4 being within the A major triad might tip the scales in favor of using the A/C♯ chord here.

- In measure 2 on beat 1, the bass and melody notes of B and D form two-thirds of both the B minor and G major triads. We could use either of these triads (the G triad would need to be inverted over its own 3rd in the bass, i.e., G/B).

- In measure 2 on beat 3, the bass and melody notes of A and F♯ form two-thirds of both the D major and F♯ minor triads. We could use either of these triads, inverted over A in the bass (i.e., either D/A or F♯m/A). Here, the melody note C♯ on beat 4 being within the F♯ minor triad suggests the F♯m/A chord as a better choice in simpler styles.

- In measure 3 on beat 1, the bass and melody notes of G and B form two-thirds of a G major triad. The primary triad is a good choice here to begin the second half of this four-measure phrase. This interval is also within the E minor triad, but inverting this triad over its own 3rd (i.e., Em/G) would be less typical at this point in the melodic phrase.

- In measure 3 on beat 3, the bass and melody notes of F♯ and D form two-thirds of a D major triad, and the A on beat 4 is the other note within this triad. So the D triad inverted over its own 3rd (D/F♯) is the clear choice here.

- In measure 4 on beat 1, the bass and melody notes of E and G form two-thirds of an E minor triad. Also, the melody note D on beat 4 is an available extension (7th) on this chord.

- In measure 4 on beat 3, the bass and melody notes of A and C♯ form two-thirds of an A major triad, and the E on the "&" of beat 3 is the other note within this triad. An A major chord is the obvious choice at this point.

Let's now develop these harmonization choices in a pop ballad piano style, as follows:

Track 83
Backing Track Style: Pop Ballad

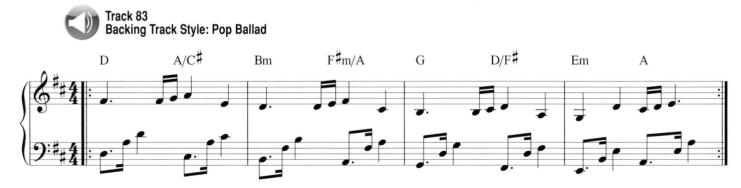

Don't forget that in piano ballad styles, you'll normally need to depress the sustain pedal for the duration of each chord (and release at the point of chord change).

The left-hand patterns here are similar to the open triad arpeggios used earlier, except that the range of each pattern is limited to one octave. This is so that the left hand stays out of the way of the melody (which is quite low, around "middle C") and yet doesn't get too "muddy" by using notes which are too low on the keyboard. Also the left-hand patterns take into account the bass inversion voicings used. Here are some comments on the individual left-hand patterns in the first two measures:

- In measure 1 on beat 1, the D–A–D pattern is the root–5th–root of the D major chord.

- In measure 1 on beat 3, the C♯–A–C♯ pattern is the 3rd–root–3rd of the A major chord inverted over its 3rd (A/C♯).

- In measure 2 on beat 1, the B–F♯–B pattern is the root–5th–root of the B minor chord.

- In measure 2 on beat 3, the A–F♯–A pattern is the 3rd–root–3rd of the F♯ minor chord inverted over its 3rd (F♯m/A).

Next, we'll look at a famous melody in the key of D minor and see how harmonization by bass line can be applied.

Melody Harmonization: "The House of the Rising Sun"

First, we'll look at an excerpt from this melody (in 3/4 time). Note that measure numbers will always exclude the pickup measure.

Track 84

Let's make some initial observations about this melody:

- The key signature is one flat, referring to either F major or D minor (which are relative to one another). Looking at this melody excerpt, we see that it both starts and ends on the note D, suggesting that this note is the tonic or for the melody, and therefore that we are in the key of D minor.

- In Chapter 3, we saw that melodies in minor keys could use different minor scales within the key (natural, harmonic, or melodic). Here we see the melody note C used in measures 6 and 10 (implying the D natural minor scale) but the melody note C♯ used in measure 14 (implying the D melodic or harmonic minor scales).

- This melody is in 3/4 time like some of the other traditional songs we've seen so far. Again, this normally means there will just be one primary beat per measure for harmonization purposes (unless the tempo is slow). So when harmonizing by bass line, we'll start out by using one bass note per measure here.

Next, we'll try to find a bass line that works with this melody. Again, we could start with the tonic of the minor key (in this case, D) and then descend. As we are in a minor key, we can try using more half steps in the bass line when descending (due to the different minor scales available in the key), as well as some larger intervals. Let's use one bass note per measure and see if useful consonant intervals are created between the melody and the bass line, as follows:

Track 85

As before, we'll go through each of these interval relationships, to determine which diatonic chords (in the key of D minor) they could imply. Again, we'll need to include bass inversions (triads inverted over their own 3rds or 5ths). Here are the most commonly used diatonic triads in the key of D minor:

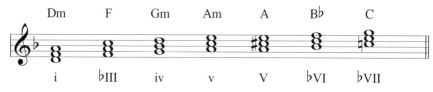

With the above triads (and their bass inversions) available, we can further analyze the harmonic implications of Track 85, as follows:

- In measure 1, the interval of D up to D is simply an octave, which can be harmonized with a D minor triad (again, a typical choice to start in this key).

- In measure 2, the bass and melody notes of C and F form two-thirds of an F major triad, and the A on beat 3 is the other note within this triad. The F triad inverted over its own 5th (F/C) is therefore a good choice here.

- In measure 3 the bass and melody notes of B and G form two-thirds of a G major triad, and the D on beat 3 is the other note within this triad. This means the G triad inverted over its own 3rd (G/B) is a good choice here.

- In measure 4, the bass and melody notes of B♭ and D form two-thirds of both the B♭ major and G minor triads. These would both be available here (the G minor triad would need to be inverted over its 3rd). Subjectively, the B♭ major triad may sound stronger following the other bass inversions.

- In measure 5, the bass and melody notes of A and D form two-thirds of a D minor triad (which would need to be inverted over its own 5th). This is a good choice here as we are halfway through the first eight-measure phrase, and the tonic chord here is helping to reinforce the minor key of the melody.

- In measure 6, the bass and melody notes of F and C form two-thirds of an F major triad, so F major is a clear choice here.

It turns out that measures 6, 7 and 8 can be viewed together here:

- We can start with measure 8 and then work backwards to see which harmonization would work best in measure 7.

- Going further back to measure 6, we can see how the left-hand bass line (from Track 85) approaches measure 7.

Next, we'll develop this working-backwards approach (from measure 8) as follows:

- Measure 8 is the last measure of the first eight-measure phrase, and in simpler styles, is likely to lead back to the tonic chord in measure 9. The strongest way to do this (with triad harmony) is to use the V major chord (A major in this case). The melody note A on beat 1 will allow this, of course. The melody note D on beat 3, while being outside this chord, is a pickup into the next melody phrase and will not prevent the A major chord from working in this measure.

- In measure 7, the E in the bass leads strongly into the A root note of the next measure, in a circle of 5ths manner. The interval of E up to A is two-thirds of an A major triad, which we can then invert over its own 5th. We now end up with essentially the same chord in measures 7–8 but with different bass notes, which adds movement and interest to the harmonization.

- In measure 6, the bass note F (see Track 85) was a subjective choice below the C in the melody. This leads into (or approaches) the following E bass note in measure 7 by a half step. This is a strong leading interval to use in the bass line.

Continuing from measure 9, we can observe the following:

- The harmonic circumstances (and resulting harmonization) in measures 9–13 are substantially similar to measures 1–5.

- In measure 14, the bass and melody notes of A and C♯ form two-thirds of an A major triad, so A major is the clear choice (particularly as it leads back strongly to the following tonic chord).

- In measures 15–16, the interval of D up to D is again simply an octave (as in measure 1). This can be harmonized with the tonic D minor triad to finish (resolve) this complete melodic phrase.

Here's a basic piano arrangement of the previous harmonization, with some partial left-hand arpeggio patterns added to give some more motion:

Track 86
Backing Track Style: 3/4 Pop

Have fun experimenting with bass line harmonization. This is an important technique which is used across a range of contemporary music styles!

PARALLEL MOTION HARMONIZATION

Finally, in this chapter, we'll look at the *parallel harmonization* technique. This can be useful when harmonizing chromatic melodies in jazzier styles. Let's take a look at a melody that we can harmonize in this manner.

Track 87

This melody is written with no key signature, as there is no discernible tonic or "home base." Also note that this melody starts with a two-measure phrase, which is then transposed up a minor 3rd interval. All of this frequently occurs in contemporary jazz styles.

Parallel harmonization occurs when the "melody-to-chord" relationship stays the same throughout a section of the melody (or sometimes the whole melody). In other words, the melody notes have the same chord function (for example, the 9th or 11th) within successive chords. The best chord qualities for this type of harmonization are normally either major, minor, or suspended dominant. This is because these chord types are not "leading" and don't need to be resolved in a particular way to the following chord.

We'll now combine this concept with the upper triad voicings developed in the last chapter, using the following steps:

1. Harmonize each melody note with a major triad in root position in the right hand.

2. Build that triad from the 7th of a suspended dominant chord (as in Track 53, measure 14).

This will result in each melody note being the 11th (or 4th) of the suspended dominant; this is commonly done in tunes by contemporary jazz artists such as Herbie Hancock and Freddie Hubbard. Next, we'll see this harmonization technique applied to the melody from Track 87, played in a jazz/fusion style.

Track 88
Backing Track Style: Jazz/Fusion

Next, we'll analyze some of the voicings in the first measure of this example to understand the harmonization technique used overall.

- In measure 1 on beat 1, the melody note F is harmonized with a B♭ major triad in root position (as F is the 5th of this triad). This B♭ major triad is in turn built from the 7th of the C9sus (suspended dominant 9th) chord. The combination of these techniques results in the melody note F becoming the 11th of the overall C9sus chord. See similar voicings in measures 8, 14, and 22 of Track 53 for other suspended dominant 9th chords.

- In measure 1 on the "&" of beat 2 (anticipating beat 3), the melody note G is harmonized with a C major triad, again in root position (as G is the 5th of this triad). This C major triad is in turn built from the 7th of the D9sus (suspended dominant 9th) chord. The combination of these techniques results in the melody note G becoming the 11th of the overall D9sus chord.

The same harmonization technique has then been applied to all of the melody notes longer than half a beat (i.e., longer than an eighth note) in Track 88 on the previous page. For example:

- The melody note B♭ (on the "&" of beat 4 in measure 1) is the 11th of the F9sus chord.

- The melody note A (on the "&" of beat 3 in measure 2) is the 11th of the E9sus chord.

We could also have harmonized the eighth notes in the melody (on beat 4 of the first and third measures) in the same way, resulting in a busier chord rhythm (greater rate of chord change). This is a matter of taste and preference, although in most cases, these shorter notes would not be separately harmonized, particularly at medium-to-fast tempos.

Now let's take the same melody, and this time, harmonize each melody note (longer than half a beat) as the 9th of a suspended dominant chord. To do this, we can again use a two-stage process as follows:

1. Harmonize each melody note with a major triad, this time in second inversion (the 5th of the triad as the lowest note).

2. Build that triad from the 7th of a suspended dominant chord.

As mentioned above, this results in each melody note becoming the 9th of a suspended dominant chord, as follows:

Track 89
Backing Track Style: Jazz/Fusion

Again, we'll analyze some of the voicings in the first measure of this example to understand the harmonization technique used overall.

- In measure 1 on beat 1, the melody note F is harmonized with a D♭ major triad in second inversion (as F is the 3rd of this triad). This D♭ major triad is in turn "built from" the 7th of the E♭9sus (suspended dominant 9th) chord. The combination of these techniques results in the melody note F becoming the 9th of the overall E♭9sus chord.

- In measure 1 on the "&" of beat 2, the melody note G is harmonized with an E♭ major triad, again in second inversion (as G is the 3rd of this triad). This E♭ major triad is in turn built from the 7th of the F9sus (suspended dominant 9th) chord. The combination of these techniques results in the melody note G becoming the 9th of the overall F9sus chord.

The same harmonization technique has then been applied to all the other significant melody notes in Track 89 on the previous page. For example:

- The melody note B♭ (on the "&" of beat 4 in measure 1) is the 9th of the A♭9sus chord.

- The melody note A (on the "&" of beat 3 in measure 2) is the 9th of the G9sus chord.

In general, the quality of a suspended dominant chord is well-suited for the type of harmonization used in Tracks 88–89. This is because it doesn't require any specific resolution to the following chord and therefore carries a more contemporary, open sound. For a famous example of suspended dominant chords moved around in a similar way, check out the classic jazz tune, "Maiden Voyage," by Herbie Hancock.

CHAPTER 6
MELODY HARMONIZATION EXAMPLES

MELODY #1: IN E♭ MAJOR

This is a basic melody which will be suitable for primary triad (I, IV, and V) harmonization. First, we'll see the melody-only notation as follows:

In basic rock or country styles, we can see if melody notes on beat 1 (or its anticipation) in consecutive measures are within the same primary triad. If so, we could use this triad for both measures, resulting in a "one chord every two measures" chord rhythm. This is useful in simpler styles, particularly at faster tempos.

For example, the G (measure 1 on beat 1) and B♭ (measure 1 on the "&" of beat 4, anticipating beat 1 of measure 2) are both within the tonic I triad (E♭ major in this key). Similarly, in measures 3–4 the C and E♭ are both within the IV triad (A♭), and so on. This harmonization can then be stylized in a classic country/pop piano style, as shown in the next example and accompanying tracks:

 Track 90
Backing Track Style: Classic Country/Pop

This has the piano styling (notated below) on the right channel, with a country/pop rhythm section on the left channel.

Track 91
Melody and Drums only (for you to experiment)

This has just the melody only on the right channel and the drums only on the left channel. With this, you can experiment with your own harmonizations while playing along to the melody and the drum part!

Here, we see triads inverted below the melody in the right hand, together with a basic root-and-5th, left-hand pattern, common in basic country and pop piano styles.

MELODY #2: IN A MAJOR

This is a slightly busier melody, which is still diatonic to the major key (A major in this case), and would therefore be suitable for diatonic triad harmonization. Again, we'll just look at the melody first, shown in the following example:

In lively contemporary styles, we'll again be looking for opportunities to use the "one chord every two measures" chord rhythm (see comments for Melody #1) where the melody allows. Otherwise, we'll aim to change chords in successive measures (i.e., one chord per measure) using the diatonic triad options developed in Chapter 2. Using more diatonic chords beyond the basic I, IV, and V (i.e., adding the minor triads) gives us more choices and available colors and is typical of most contemporary pop/rock styles.

One of various possible diatonic triad harmonization options (in A major), arranged in a pop/rock piano style, is shown below and on the next page.

Track 92
Backing Track Style: Modern Pop/Rock

Track 93
Melody and Drums only (for you to experiment)

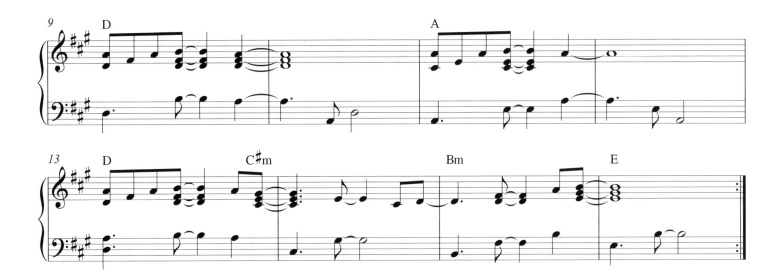

Again, we see triads below the melody in the right hand (a staple device across a range of pop piano styles), some with *octave doubling* (an octave interval between the top and bottom notes) and with some anticipations as dictated by the melody. The left hand is playing a more active pattern with roots and 5ths of chords coupled with anticipations (i.e., of beat 3 in some measures). All this is common in mainstream pop/rock piano styles.

MELODY #3: IN E MINOR

Next, we have a minor key melody which uses a 16th-note rhythmic subdivision and anticipations. If you need to, refer to Chapter 2 regarding chord rhythms for 16th-note melodies and harmonization in minor keys. Here's the melody before any harmonization is applied:

As discussed in Chapter 2, in 16th-note styles, we'll normally need to ensure that our chords work with melody notes landing on all of the downbeats or their anticipations (see text accompanying Track 46).

In slow- to mid-tempo, 16th-note pop styles, we'll most often need at least a "one chord per measure" chord rhythm for stylistic interest, and we'll frequently go to "two chords per measure" to accommodate the melody and/or to add more harmonic movement.

Although some slower-tempo ballads will sometimes need more frequent chord changes (i.e., on successive beats) to accommodate the melody, it's recommended that you keep this to a minimum. Busy chord rhythms can be too distracting. It's a judgement call!

The melodic and rhythmic style of Melody #3 suggests a more sophisticated R&B/pop treatment beyond simple diatonic triads in the minor key. So in the harmonization, we've used some upper triad voicings (as in Tracks 39, 53, etc.) as well as bass inversions (as in Tracks 57, 80, etc.), as follows:

Track 94
Backing Track Style: R&B/Pop Ballad

Track 95
Melody and Drums only (for you to experiment)

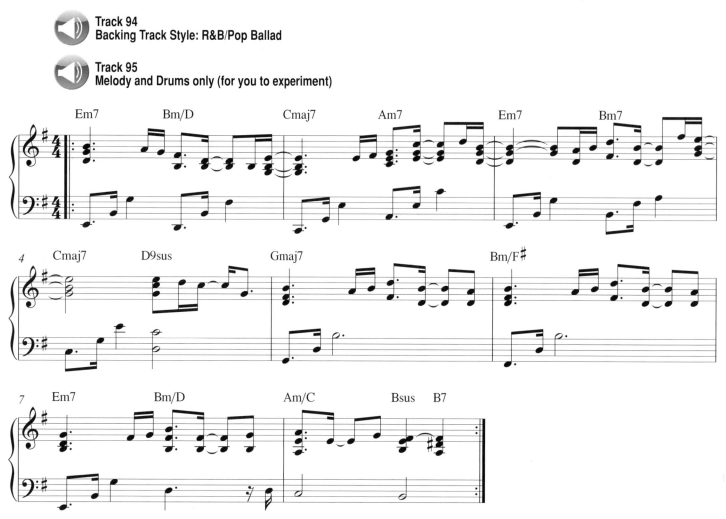

Let's analyze the right-hand triads below the melody in the first two measures of this harmonization:

- In measure 1 on beat 1, the G major triad is built from the 7th of the Em7 chord.

- In measure 1 during beat 3, the right-hand notes (B and F sharp) form two-thirds of a B minor triad that is inverted over its own 3rd in the bass.

- In measure 2 on beat 1, the E minor triad is built from the 5th of the Cmaj7 chord.

- In measure 2 on beat 3, the C major triad is built from the 3rd of the Am7 chord.

The left hand is often playing open triad arpeggio patterns as seen earlier, with a 16th-note pickup into beats 2 and/or 4 (known as the *backbeats*). The right-hand triads are sometimes anticipating the downbeats, as dictated by the melody. All this is typical of R&B ballad piano styles.

MELODY #4: IN D (MAJOR-MINOR MIX)

Our next melody again uses 16th-note subdivisions and anticipations, this time combining notes from both the D major and D natural minor scales. Here's the melody before any harmonization is applied:

The key signature is for D major, so the melody notes from the D natural minor scale (i.e., the C in measure 1, the F in measure 2, and so on) require accidentals in the music (in this case, natural signs to cancel out the sharps in the key signature; see Track 78 and accompanying text). Also, note the *courtesy* accidentals at the start of measures 3 and 5. These are present to remind us that we are expected to play F♯ in the melody (from the D major scale) in those measures.

When harmonizing this D "major-minor mix" melody, the starting point would be to use the common diatonic triads from both scales, as follows:

- D major (i.e., D, Em, F♯m, G, A, Bm).

- D minor (i.e., Dm, F, Gm, Am, B♭, C).

A similar example of combining triads, this time using the C major-minor mix, can be seen before Track 78 in Chapter 4.

The following harmonization just uses triads from the above options, without using any upper triad or bass inversion voicings (of the type we saw in Melody #3). In other words, we've limited ourselves to basic major and minor triads throughout, although you're welcome to try some alternatives! The melodic styling uses a swing-16th rhythmic subdivision, which is colloquially referred to as a funk shuffle or half-time shuffle. The swing-16th rhythmic style divides pairs of 16th notes in a two-thirds to one-third ratio, rather than exactly "half and half" as with regular (straight) 16ths. For much more information on swing-16ths rhythmic styles and funk styles in general, please see our *Pop Piano Book*, *Rock Piano Chops,* and *Jazz-Rock Piano Chops* book, all published by Hal Leonard.

> The example appears on the next page for easier reading.

Here, the piano styling uses triads or partial triads below the melody in the right hand, following the anticipations as in earlier examples.

The left hand is playing the root of each chord at the points of chord change (i.e., the primary beats 1 and 3), and is either:

- Landing on the backbeats (i.e., 2 and 4) if that coincides with a rest in the melody (for example beat 4 of measure 1, beat 4 of measure 4, etc.).

or:

- Anticipating the backbeats if the right hand is landing on that beat (for example, beat 2 of measures 1 and 2, beat 4 of measure 3, etc.).

All this creates an interesting rhythmic conversation between the right- and left-hand parts, which is typical of funk keyboard styles.

MELODY #5: NO KEY SIGNATURE (CHROMATIC MELODY)

For the last melody example in this chapter, we return to an eighth-note subdivision and feel, this time without a key signature as we are not working within a major or minor scale restriction, and there is no discernible "tonic" (see Track 87 and accompanying text). This type of chromatic melody is often found in contemporary jazz and fusion styles. Again, we'll start with the melody first before choosing the harmonization.

This type of chromatic melody will often repeat (or *sequence*) small melodic motifs, transposing by different intervals. For example, the melodic motif in measures 5–8 is the same as in measures 1–4, but transposed up either an augmented 2nd or minor 3rd interval. Also, the melodic motif in measures 11–12 is substantially similar to measures 9–10, but transposed down a major 2nd (whole step) interval. This is very common in certain jazz and funk melodic styles.

For this chromatic melody, we'll try using parallel harmonization with suspended dominant 9th chords (similar to Tracks 88 and 89 from Chapter 6).

Track 98
Backing Track Style: Jazz/Fusion

Track 99
Melody and Drums only (for you to experiment)

- In measures 1–8, each melody note is harmonized with a root-position triad in the right hand. This is in turn built from the 7th of a suspended dominant 9th chord (with the left hand playing the root and 5th of the chord). This results in each melody note in this section becoming the 11th (or 4th) of each suspended dominant chord, respectively.

This is the same parallel harmonization technique used for Track 88.

- In measures 9–12, each melody note is harmonized with a second inversion triad in the right hand. This is built from the 7th of a suspended dominant 9th chord (with the left hand playing the root and 7th of the chord). This results in each melody note in this section becoming the 9th of each suspended dominant chord, respectively.

This is the parallel harmonization technique used for Track 89.

All this gives a very recognizable, contemporary jazz/fusion feel to the harmonization. As usual, you are encouraged to experiment!